At the Top of Their Game

LeBron James
King of the Court

Rachel Shuster

Cavendish Square

New York

Published in 2018 by Cavendish Square Publishing, LLC
243 5th Avenue, Suite 136, New York, NY 10016
Copyright © 2018 by Cavendish Square Publishing, LLC

First Edition

CPSIA Compliance Information: Batch #CS17CSQ

All websites were available and accurate when this book was sent to press.

Library of Congress Cataloging-in-Publication Data

Names: Shuster, Rachel, author.
Title: LeBron James : king of the court / Rachel Shuster.
Description: New York : Cavendish Square Publishing, 2018. | Series: At the
top of their game | Includes bibliographical references and index.
Identifiers: LCCN 2016051650 (print) | LCCN 2016052604 (ebook) | ISBN
9781502628367 (library bound) | ISBN 9781502628374 (E-book)
Subjects: LCSH: James, LeBron. | Basketball players--United
States--Biography--Juvenile literature. | African American basketball
players--Biography--Juvenile literature.
Classification: LCC GV884.J36 S497 2018 (print) | LCC GV884.J36 (ebook) | DDC
796.323--dc23
LC record available at HYPERLINK "https://lccn.loc.gov/2016051650" https://lccn.loc.
gov/2016051650

Editorial Director: David McNamara
Editor: Fletcher Doyle
Copy Editor: Rebecca Rohan
Associate Art Director: Amy Greenan
Designer: Jessica Nevins
Production Coordinator: Karol Szymczuk
Photo Research: J8 Media

The photographs in this book are used by permission and through the courtesy of: Cover Ezra Shaw/
Getty Images; p. 4 Miami Herald/Tribune News Service/Getty Images; p. 8 Stacey Lynn Payne/
Shutterstyock.com; p. 13 Al Tielemans/Sports Illustrated/Getty Images; p. 16 Justin Jay/Getty
Images; pp. 19, 22, 26, 30, 33, 42, 48, 50, 71, 76, 82, 88 ©AP Images; p. 24 Courtesy of
Patty Burdon/St. Vincent – St. Mary High School; p. 33 Sporting News Archive/Getty Images; p.
52 Gustavo Caballero/WireImage/Getty Images; p. 55 REUTERS/Alamy Stock Photo; p. 60 David
Santiago/El Nuevo Herald/©AP Images; p. 64 Angelo Merendino/Getty Images; p. 73 epa european
pressphoto agency b.v./Alamy Stock Photo; p. 84 WENN Ltd/Alamy Stock Photo; p. 93 Mary
Cybulski/©Universal Pictures/courtesy Everett Collection.

Printed in the United States of America

At the Top of Their Game

Contents

Introduction...5

Chasing a Ghost

Chapter 1...9

Mr. Basketball

Chapter 2...27

Making of a Superstar

Chapter 3...43

Leaving Home

Chapter 4...65

Redemption

Chapter 5...83

More Than Just Basketball

Timeline...98

Glossary...100

Bibliography...103

Further Information...106

Index...109

About the Author...112

Chasing a Ghost

For a generation of basketball fans who believed no one would approach the likes of Michael Jordan again, yet who termed every rising star "the next Michael Jordan" and who heaped such pressure on those rising stars that no one could possibly live up to the expectations—LeBron James confounded and dazzled and disheartened and amazed right from the start of his still-rising, **enigmatic** career.

From the time he was three years old and wouldn't play with his toy basketball set unless the hoop was placed on the highest setting, James has known only one thing—to go all-out. That drive sustained him through a childhood without a father; through entering the NBA at nineteen and earning Rookie of the Year honors; and through early stardom in Cleveland but failure to bring the Cavaliers a title. It got him through the ridicule of saying on live TV that he was "taking his talents to South Beach" to play for the Miami Heat, then seeing his likeness burning **in effigy** by his former fans in Cleveland. And it humbled him when in 2016 he finally did

Opposite: LeBron James was exuberant after leading the Miami Heat to victory against the Oklahoma Thunder for the 2012 NBA title, his first after nine seasons in the league.

deliver a championship for Cleveland as a returning Cavalier, the city's first sports title of any kind in more than fifty years.

Today, LeBron James has reached the pinnacle of his basketball career, but he is not satisfied. "My motivation is this ghost I'm chasing. The ghost played in Chicago," James said, comparing himself to Jordan in a *Sports Illustrated* interview in August 2016, just months after his third NBA title.

Away from the court, he has done much for the community in the Cleveland area, particularly in his nearby hometown of Akron, Ohio. He has done things particularly for the youth, but he is not satisfied in that arena, either. Perhaps both feelings come from an inner place where being satisfied was not an option. Not when he had the example of his mother and all she would do to make life better for her children.

"My mom, she set me up for the life I have now," said James, who has his mom's name tattooed on his arm, in an interview with WebMD in April 2010.

"I had my mother to blanket me, to give me security. [When I was] growing up, she was my mother, my father, everything. To grow up in a single-parent household, to see what she could do all by herself, that gave me a lot of strength."

Strength is a good word to associate with James, both on and off the basketball court. On the court, his monster dunks, his ability to power through multiple defenders flailing every which way at him, and his chase-down blocks that thunder through the arena and right through your TV screen, have been his calling cards in a career that includes three NBA championships and appearances in the last six NBA Finals.

Off the court, his strength of character comes through in his numerous activities to make life better for those less fortunate. Whether it's providing college scholarships for at-risk youth or business opportunities for would-be **entrepreneurs**, James has become one of those rare athletes whose vision extends beyond the field of play.

Today, visitors to his high school, St. Vincent-St. Mary in Akron, can watch basketball games in LeBron James Arena, which seats almost two thousand fans. In 2012, after winning his first NBA title, James returned home and pledged $1 million to renovate his high school arena, which was completed and ready for basketball games in December 2013.

"Just using our resources, using our strength, using everything that we've been able to do to just build up these communities," James told more than five thousand children and their families at an Ohio event in September 2016. The event kicked off the sixth year of his "Akron I Promise" program to keep youngsters on track toward educational success.

He was like many of those kids when he grew up in Akron.

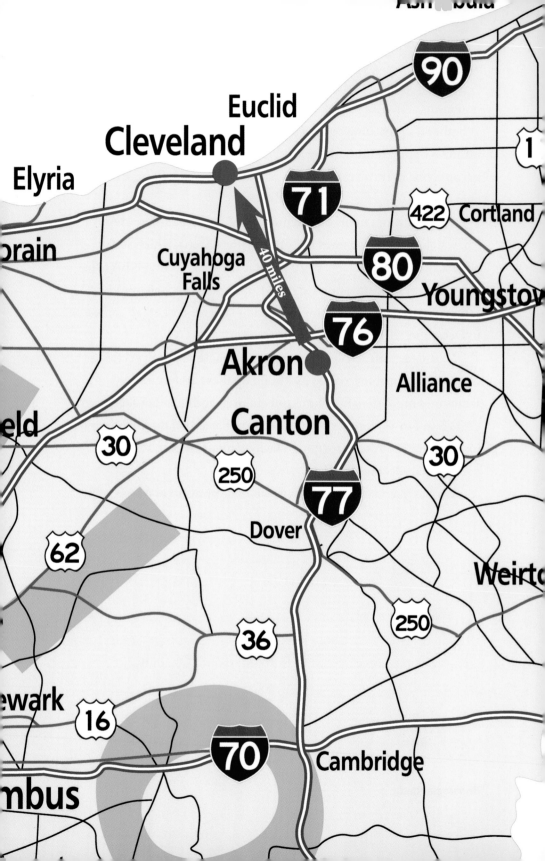

Chapter 1

Mr. Basketball

LeBron James appreciates that his early years in the inner city, growing up without a father, could have derailed what has become a storybook life. But he uses that as motivation, as in this imaginary conversation with his dad that he once posted on Instagram:

> Like, Wow, Dad, you know what, I don't know you, I have no idea who you are, but because of you is part of the reason who I am today. The fuel that I use—you not being there—it's part of the reason I grew up to become who I am. It's part of the reason I want to be hands-on with my endeavors … So me in a position allowing people around me to grow, that maybe wouldn't have happened if I had two parents, two sisters, a dog, and a picket fence, you know?

His mother was sixteen when James was born. His grandmother, Freda, helped raised him while his mother went back to school. They lived with four generations of family in a

Opposite: James grew up in Akron, Ohio, 40 miles (64 kilometers) southeast of Cleveland, where his NBA career began with the Cavaliers.

big house on a dirt road near the railroad tracks of Akron. On the Christmas morning when James was three, his grandmother died of a heart attack at forty-two. The family fell apart as bills went unpaid, including heat for the house. Dirty dishes piled up; holes developed in the floors. A neighbor offered to let them come and live at her house. It was the first of what would be dozens of moves over the next five years. James had to grow up fast.

"I had to be there and do things that probably a father would do," James recalled in a 2016 interview with Cleveland.com. "Obviously, not to that magnitude because I wasn't a grownup and I didn't have responsibilities, but I had to handle myself and make sure I wasn't a problem to my mother so she didn't have to have extra things going on in her head, because she had a lot on her plate already."

And when he did give his mom a little trouble?

"Hell yeah, I heard it from her," James said. "She'd say, 'Boy, you ain't grown.' I heard that many times."

He switched schools constantly. He would be alone at night while his mom went to work, or, after she had lost a job, when she would go out to party. "Sometimes I went to bed not knowing if I was going to see her in the morning," he wrote in *Shooting Stars*, his autobiography.

Finding a Friend

When he was seven, they were about to be evicted from another housing project when local football coach Bruce Kelker asked if James wanted to join his team, the East Dragons. That is where James met Frankie Walker Jr., the son of one of the coaches. James went over to the Walker house on Christmas and ended up staying there the rest of the school break.

John Reed was the basketball coach of the Summit Lake Hornets when the elder Walker introduced eight-year-old James to him. Reed would leave his construction job at 4:00 p.m. each day and swing around to pick up any players needing a ride to practice. James never knew where he would be from day to day, so he would leave messages on Reed's answering machine saying where to pick him up.

Reed made everyone play all the positions, the root of the skills James counts on today as an oversized point guard or undersized center—he's now six feet eight inches and 250 pounds (2 meters and 113 kilograms)—when called on by his NBA coaches. Passing, in particular, was emphasized. Team-first basketball.

Growing into a Player

When he was nine, James went to live full-time with Frank and Pamela Walker. He shared a room with Frankie Jr., and the boys had posters of Michael Jordan and Allen Iverson on the walls. Basketball became a true obsession for James, who loved the pace of the game. James used every opportunity he could to practice, whether against players his age and size or older and taller. He would even challenge Reed to a game of one-on-one, and one time he predicted that would be the night he would finally beat the coach. They went shot for shot, until Reed finally missed—and James didn't. "I'm going to the NBA," were James's parting words, Reed recalled.

It was also around that time that James first met the man he described in his autobiography as "the most special" he has ever met, "with a heart that was beautiful and bountiful, Dru Joyce II—otherwise known to all as Coach Dru—and his son, Dru Joyce III, aka, Little Dru."

By the sixth grade, James six feet (1.8 meters) tall, could play all five positions on the basketball court and had a sixth sense for the game. Dru Joyce coached the Northeast Ohio Shooting Stars, an Amateur Athletic Union (AAU) basketball team. With Little Dru, Sian Cotton, Willie McGee, and James all playing together, the Shooting Stars qualified in 1997 for the AAU Sixth Grade National Championships in Salt Lake City, Utah. To help pay for the trip, the boys went door-to-door asking for donations. They collected enough money to buy plane tickets. James admitted he "cried like there was no tomorrow" as he sat "scared out of my wits" through his first plane ride. They finished tenth overall.

Two years later, determined to achieve their dream of winning a national title, the Shooting Stars made it all the way to the AAU Eighth Grade National Championships in Orlando, Florida. Aided by James, at six feet two inches and able to dunk the ball, the Shooting Stars won their first five games to set up a showdown with the Southern California All-Stars, a team James described as having swagger and treating the kids from Akron like "bumpkins from Hicksville USA who still had outhouses." The Shooting Stars got behind by fifteen points early but rallied and had a shot at the lead with just seconds to play. James attempted a three-point shot from 35 feet (10.7 m) away, and the ball went in—then "popped" out. They lost by two points, a memory that still haunts James.

The "Fab Four"

Was that the end of their journey? Hardly. James, Little Dru, Cotton, and McGee—the self-proclaimed "Fab Four"—had arrived at a decision. ("Decision" would become an even more meaningful word to James after he turned pro.) They were a package deal—get them

LeBron James's basketball career took flight at Akron's St. Vincent-St. Mary High School, a Catholic school previously known for its academic excellence.

all into one high school, or get none of them. The sting of the AAU loss was the motivating force, because they all believed they were destined for something great.

The foursome settled on St. Vincent-St. Mary High School (SVSM), a private Catholic school in downtown Akron, known for academic excellence, not athletic excellence. The African American community was not pleased. But SVSM represented the best place for all four to get a chance to play, including the five-foot (1.5 m) Little Dru.

Starting as a freshman, James scored fifteen points and grabbed eight rebounds in his first game. The SVSM Fighting Irish would go on to win the state championship in their first season, with senior Maverick Carter (who would become one of James' closest friends) as captain. When Carter graduated, the Fab Four needed another player for their sophomore season, and it came in the form of transfer student Romeo Travis.

The high school had moved its home games to the five-thousand-seat University of Akron gym—James A. Rhodes Arena, commonly called "the JAR"—when James was a sophomore. This was done to accommodate the number of fans wanting to see him play. The place sold out immediately, even with season-ticket packages for the Fighting Irish costing $125.

James and his team backed up that first title by winning another in his sophomore season. James made the *USA Today* All-USA First Team, the first sophomore to achieve that distinction.

James began the summer after his sophomore year in Colorado Springs, Colorado, at the USA Basketball Development Festival. The first underclassman ever invited to the camp, he broke the festival scoring record with 120 points in five games and was named Most Valuable Player.

It was also around this time that James met his future wife, Savannah Brinson, who attended a rival high school in Akron. She was a softball player and a cheerleader, but she had no idea of the enormity of James's fame. According to *Harper's Bazaar* magazine, he spotted her at a football game and asked her to come to a basketball game. Their first official date was at a steakhouse. "I knew he loved me when I left my leftovers from dinner in his car," she told the magazine. "I'd totally forgotten about them, and he brought them to me. I think he just wanted another excuse to come and see me."

Never did she imagine the life the two of them would have. "I just thought he'd be a hometown hero for his era and it would be over," she told *Harper's Bazaar*.

As a junior in 2002 and a senior in 2003, James was named *Parade* High School Basketball Player of the Year, the first repeat winner, as well as the Gatorade Player of the Year and *USA Today* high school basketball player of the year for both seasons.

SVSM Rockets to Fame

Before James's junior season, his first coach, Keith Dambrot, moved on to the University of Akron as an assistant. This left the door open for his assistant, Coach Dru, to become SVSM's first African American head coach.

Coach Dru walked into a situation in which his best player was not just a state star but was growing a national reputation for his unique skills. Interest in James was so widespread that some of his high school games were shown on pay-per-view cable in parts of Ohio.

"He's the best high school player I've ever seen, " wrote *Akron Beacon Journal* sports columnist Terry Pluto. "I'm very guarded

Dubbed "The Chosen One" by *Sports Illustrated* during his high school career, James chose to make it a lasting impression.

about saying that, because the last thing he needs is more hype. But I have never seen a better one."

Sports Illustrated crowned him "The Chosen One" for the cover of its Feb. 18, 2002, edition. (He later had "CHOSEN 1" tattooed across his back.) That escalated the attention. Reporters clamored to get into practices. James was hounded for autographs wherever he went. Parents were sending their kids to him to get the cover autographed—then turning around and selling the signed copy on eBay. In fact, the team lost the very first game after the cover story appeared and went on to lose in the state championship.

They had been winning but also partying and misbehaving and generally not listening to Coach Dru. That all changed as they entered their senior year, the goal of a national championship staring at them for one last time. In a team meeting in the locker room before the first practice of the season, their commitment to each other was reinforced—as well as to their coach. As James wrote in *Shooting Stars*:

> We were angry. We were ashamed of the year before. We were inspired by *USA Today*'s preseason national rankings, which placed St. V twenty-third in the nation. We viewed that as a slap—and a spur. We were better than that. Now we had to prove it.

Before James's senior season, SVSM struck a deal to broadcast all ten of its home games throughout northeast Ohio on pay-per-view at $7.95 a pop, available in 600,000 homes and fourteen counties. Their top-notch schedule also took them all over the country, and they were the biggest of draws: 8,722 at Philadelphia's Palestra; 12,500 at UCLA's Pauley Pavilion; 15,000 at the Greensboro (NC)

Coliseum. They were rock stars, and James was the biggest. *The Late Show with David Letterman, The Oprah Winfrey Show* and *Live with Regis and Kelly* were among the very popular national TV shows asking (and being turned down) for James to appear.

The team got off to a 2-0 start, then faced its nemesis, the nation's number-one-ranked team. Virginia's Oak Hill Academy had beaten the Fab Four by one point in their sophomore season and by six points in their junior season. Oak Hill, as usual, was loaded with players headed to Division I colleges and entered the game with a 7-0 record.

Except this time, the matchup would be televised.

Breaking into the Big Time

ESPN2 agreed to televise the December 2002 contest at the 13,600-seat Convocation Center on the campus of Cleveland State—and brought in the big guns to announce it, including Dick Vitale and

A highlight of LeBron James's high school career was a 65-45 victory in December 2002 vs. number-one-ranked Oak Hill, carried live by ESPN2.

Naismith Memorial Basketball Hall of Famer Bill Walton. They got their money's worth, as SVSM defeated Oak Hill, 65-45, with James going off for thirty-one points on twelve-for-twenty-five shooting, with thirteen rebounds and six assists in thirty-two minutes of play. A staggering 1.67 million households tuned into the game and 11,523 fans were in the stands, with tickets going for as much as $100 courtside.

"I came here with high expectations," said Walton, who had asked if he could announce the game to see James up close. "I'm leaving more impressed than I could have ever believed. This guy has the complete package. What I saw tonight was a special basketball player. It was an eye-opening experience for me."

Added Vitale: "His understanding of how to play, his explosiveness, his size, and his passing ability—he's so **reminiscent** of Magic (Johnson). Like only the very special players, he has the unique ability to make people around him better."

Their enthusiasm for James was lambasted in the media, with reporters calling Walton and Vitale **shills** for the network. Looking back on that time for *Esquire* in 2016, Vitale had the last laugh.

> When the game started, I couldn't believe what I was watching. I turned to Bill, and I remember saying this on the air: "My friend, I'm telling you up and down: This kid is better than advertised. Better. He will be an instant star." And it's been unbelievable watching him go, and he's just been off the charts.

The victory boosted SVSM to ninth in the national polls. The next big test came against Los Angeles's Mater Dei High School, ranked fourth. The game was held on the campus of UCLA. The hype was over the top even for a LeBron James event: the team was picked up in a stretch limo at the airport, scalpers were selling tickets for two or three times face value, fans were buying merchandise with James's face on it, and towels at the hotel read "St. Mary-St. Vincent."

Tied at 11-11 after the first quarter, the team pulled it together, withstood a late Mater Dei charge, and won, 64-58. Suddenly, they were the number-one-ranked team in the nation.

Talking to a *Dallas Morning News* reporter, SVSM headmaster David Rathz marveled how James still fit in with the others at school, some going on to college while he seemed certain to be headed for a multimillion-dollar career in the NBA. "Here he is, this much higher than everyone else. I don't know why he isn't an egomaniac," Rathz said then. "He's down to earth, has fun with his friends, goes to class, has the grades," including a 3.5 grade-point average during the first nine-week period of his final school year.

Time to Say Goodbye

The celebration after the victory over Mater Dei and the number-one ranking was short-lived. For James's eighteenth birthday, on December 30, 2002, his mother bought him a Hummer. The base price was around $50,000, but tricked out with three televisions and a video game system, its cost was more like $100,000. As James wrote, that price tag "was far more than our net worth, because we didn't have any net worth." His mother had taken out a bank loan, which was questioned by the national media. But she produced documentation, and a two-week investigation by the Ohio High School Athletic Association (OHSAA) concluded there was no hidden third party trying to curry favor with the James family. That didn't stop the scrutiny. But pressure? Not for James, who wrote:

Controversy followed James after his mother bought him an expensive eighteenth birthday present: a tricked-out Hummer costing $100,000, raising questions about his continued eligibility to play for St. Vincent-St. Mary.

Pressure was being born without a father to a mother who was sixteen. Pressure was watching the house that had belonged to the family get condemned by the city and torn down, leaving my mother and me with no place to live. Pressure was staying up half the night worrying if my mom was okay. Pressure was moving from place to place and from school to school. Hummer Hysteria was no kind of pressure to me.

The team kept winning, remaining undefeated. James kept making headlines away from the basketball court. While shopping at a Cleveland clothing store in January 2003, James was offered two throwback sports jerseys, of former Baltimore Bullets star center Wes Unseld and former Chicago Bears Hall of Famer Gale Sayers. He posed for pictures with the jerseys, valued at $845, to be displayed in the store. Innocent enough, right? Except a story in the (Cleveland) *Plain Dealer* caught the attention of the OHSAA, which did another investigation and ruled that James had violated the rule forbidding receiving free gifts of value because of his fame as an athlete. He was declared ineligible for the rest of the season.

"It was a witch hunt," Headmaster Rathz said at the time. "They wanted to get [James] and get the school."

James was inconsolable, but there was Coach Dru, telling him if this was the worst that would happen to him in his life, then he will have lived "a pretty good life." And the rest of the team stepped up and won their first game without him by one point to remain unbeaten.

The family retained an attorney, who filed a temporary restraining order and preliminary injunction to prevent the OHSAA

St. Vincent-St. Mary fans now attend games at LeBron James Arena.

from revoking James's eligibility. It worked. A Summit County judge ruled James ineligible for one additional game but otherwise reinstated. St. Vincent-St. Mary also had to forfeit one victory. His first game back, James scored a career-high fifty-two points in a 78-52 victory against Los Angeles-based Westchester High in the Prime Time Shootout in New Jersey. After the game, James told reporters: "Maybe if something else comes up, I'll score fifty-two again." The additional game he sat out was the last of the regular season, which the team won.

Four victories later, the SVSM team was the state champion and the national champion.

> We had accomplished our goal and dream, and ... we had done it in the last game of basketball we would ever play together. ... It was hard not to think how lucky I had been to have the love of the Walkers and then find a father figure in Coach Dru. ... It was hard not to think how important it was that we stuck together as one when the black community of Akron accused us of being traitors for not going to public school. ... But it was also hard not to think that we *would* go our separate ways in just a few months.

Dru Joyce III and Romeo Travis each starred at the University of Akron and played pro basketball overseas. Willie McGee is athletic director at SVSM. Sian Cotton went on to a musical career as a rapper. Another member of that 2003 team, Brandon Weems, is a college scout for the Cavaliers.

James considered going to college, and the schools that made his list included North Carolina, Duke, Florida, Ohio State, and Louisville. However, even college coaches told him "not to waste" his time spending a season playing NCAA basketball. So on April 25, 2003, LeBron James declared himself eligible for the NBA draft.

"When you see there's no way you can get any hotter ... you've got to take on an opportunity when it's in front of you, and that's what made me make this decision," James said in announcing his decision at SVSM. "I'm just looking forward to the challenge. I love challenges. And I know everyone's going to be coming after me."

Chapter 2

Making of a Superstar

The NBA's Cleveland Cavaliers were well acquainted with James— he even had cost them. In May 2002, the Cavs were fined $150,000 and head coach John Lucas was suspended for the first two games of the next season for inviting James, a player not yet eligible for the draft, to work out with the team. James's turn would come a year later.

Indeed, everyone remembers the night of the 2003 NBA draft, June 26, at New York's Madison Square Garden (MSG), when the world of the Cavaliers turned into the whirlwind associated with one LeBron James. However, the real fate of the Cavaliers was determined thirty-five days earlier, when the NBA gathered seven miles and one river away from MSG, in Secaucus, NJ, scene of the 2003 draft lottery. The lottery would determine the draft order. This was the night of perhaps the Cavaliers' biggest victory.

Cavaliers general manager Jim Paxson was at home, sitting on a couch, his heart pounding, as he and his wife watched the lottery on TV. The Denver Nuggets, even with one of the top two chances

Opposite: LeBron James was thrilled when his hometown Cleveland Cavaliers and general manager Jim Paxson, right, made him the overall top choice of the 2003 NBA draft.

to get the first overall pick, slipped to third. It came down to the Cavaliers and the Memphis Grizzlies. The Cavs ended up drawing the top pick.

"We don't know who we are going to pick," Cavaliers owner Gordon Gund joked, when interviewed.

Paxson sure knew who the team would pick. As did James.

"I'm staying in Cleveland, and I'm real excited," James said at the subsequent news conference, surrounded by his SVSM teammates. "I'm not going to guarantee a championship, but I will guarantee we'll get better every day. We're going to be a lot better than we were last year."

When it became glaringly obvious who Cleveland's number one pick would be, the flurry was on to buy season tickets. The Cavaliers had sold out only two games the previous season. But this time, the rush was so great that even James's mother was turned down from buying the seats she wanted!

What was all the excitement about? As ESPN NBA analyst Chad Ford wrote:

> Can LeBron handle the pressure of turning around the franchise? The interviews? The hype? The large target placed squarely on his chest? No one in recent history has come into the league with more talent and more expectations. If he actually lives up to it all, then we actually had him underrated as a human being.

Fortune Before the Ball Bounces

Before he even played his first regular-season game for the Cavaliers, before he was even drafted, James was already wealthy —he had signed a seven-year, $90 million contract with Nike. At the time, Reebok had future Hall of Famer Allen Iverson as an endorser from the world of basketball; adidas had Tracy McGrady. Nike had Michael Jordan, but in 2003, Jordan was finishing his last season in the NBA, with the Washington Wizards. Nike needed a new pitchman who could move its best-selling products: basketball shoes.

When Jordan, as a rookie, signed with Nike in 1984, his deal was for five years and a *total* of $2.5 million. Nike needed a 3,500 percent increase in less than twenty years to make a deal with James.

"Nike is the right fit and has the right product for me at the right time," James said in a company statement then. "They are a good company that has committed to supporting me throughout my professional career, on and off the court."

(He was on target there: in 2015, he signed a lifetime contract with Nike for reportedly more than $1 billion!)

Nike released the first shoe endorsed by James, the Air Zoom Generation, in December 2003. At $110 a pair, Nike sold 72,000 pairs worth $7.92 million in the first month alone.

As he was signing with Nike, James also signed an exclusive contract with Upper Deck trading cards for a reported $1 million a year for five years, plus a $1 million signing bonus. He was the youngest person ever signed by Upper Deck. (His rookie card, with an authentic NBA **logo** jersey patch and James's autograph, was expected to be sold for as much as $200,000 at an auction in 2016.)

Draft Night

It was the least surprising moment of the night.

"With the first pick of the 2003 NBA draft, the Cleveland

LeBron James towered over National Basketball Association Commissioner David Stern when he took the stage at New York's Madison Square Garden on draft night, June 26, 2003.

Cavaliers select … LeBron James," NBA Commissioner David Stern intoned at 7:37 p.m. (EDT) on June 26 at MSG, home of the New York Knicks.

James hugged his mother, hugged his agent, pulled on a Cavaliers cap, and strode to the stage to shake Stern's hand. He got a hint of things to come when the boisterous New York crowd booed his selection. However, it didn't seem to faze him.

"I'm one of the highest publicized players in the country right now, and I haven't even played one game of basketball in the NBA," James told reporters. "I know I'm a marked man, but I just have to go out there and play hard and play strong and help my teammates every night."

Or, as *USA Today* NBA reporter David DuPree wrote, "James is considered a can't-miss prospect with the skills of a guard, the body of a forward, and the potential of a superstar."

James topped an impressive draft class: Carmelo Anthony went third to the Nuggets, Chris Bosh went fourth to the Toronto Raptors, and Dwyane Wade went fifth to the Miami Heat, the latter two joining forces with James years later to win back-to-back championships.

For now, James saw his mission clearly: to get the Cavaliers into the playoffs for the first time since 1998.

"I wouldn't want none of the pressure," Anthony said at the time.

He wasn't LeBron James. "I think I was a God-given talent. But also, I worked to get where I'm at," James said. "The dream has finally come. … You come to Cleveland this year and see how glamorous it is. It's going to be lit up like Vegas."

At a party the Cavaliers held in Cleveland during the draft, fans cheered and hugged as James was announced as the overall first pick.

The Cavaliers were ready with wine-and-gold James jerseys on sale for $50 each.

"We appreciate the support of our fans in getting to this point where there's at least a lot more hope than we had before," said Paxson. James "has as good a floor vision as any young player that has come into the game in a long time. I think you can put the ball in his hands and ask him to do a lot of things. The biggest thing that jumped out at me is that he's a very unselfish player."

Reality "Sets In"

As described in the *Sporting News,* James made a play in his first preseason game that showed his previous coaches were correct about the youngster's uncanny passing ability. On a fast break against the Detroit Pistons, Darius Miles slipped the ball to James in the key. Without breaking stride, James made a no-look pass to Ricky Davis, who converted for a layup.

"I saw [Larry] Bird and Magic [Johnson] do that," Paxson told the *Sporting News.* "You can't teach that. Can't take credit for that one. That's a gift."

The Cavaliers did not win James's first game as a pro, but James nonetheless made all the highlight reels on October 29, 2003, with a stat line of twenty-five points, nine assists and six rebounds—at age nineteen!

James played in all but three of the team's eighty-two games and scored double-figure points in all but six. He averaged twenty-eight points in a seven-game stretch in late December and 22.6 points during a seven-game winning streak in March that was the team's longest since 1997. At the end of that month, he recorded season highs of forty-one points (including the team's final ten points) and

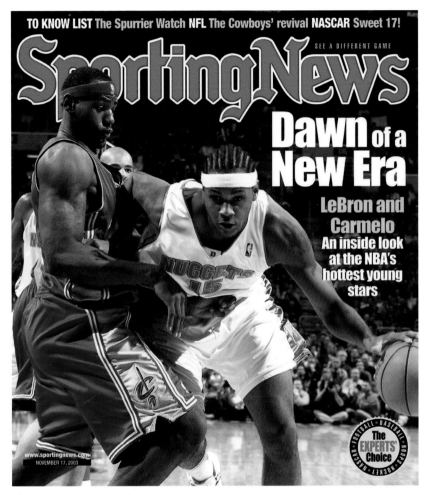

TO KNOW LIST The Spurrier Watch NFL The Cowboys' revival NASCAR Sweet 17!

SEE A DIFFERENT GAME

Sporting News

Dawn of a
New Era

LeBron and
Carmelo
An inside look
at the NBA's
hottest young
stars

www.sportingnews.com
NOVEMBER 17, 2003

The
EXPERTS'
Choice

Two of the hottest young NBA stars, LeBron James and Carmelo Anthony, would go on to become friends and play together on the US Olympic basketball team with the elite of the elite.

thirteen assists in a three-point win against the New Jersey Nets.

His play garnered James an appearance in the Rookie Challenge Game during that season's All-Star weekend, and he led the newcomers with thirty-three points in a loss to the second-year players.

Was there any doubt he would be voted Rookie of the Year, after averaging 20.9 points, 5.9 assists, and 5.5 rebounds, and leading the Cavaliers to a 35-47 record, an eighteen-game turnaround? Cleveland power forward Carlos Boozer told *Sports Illustrated,* "You can only call it court sense. The way he takes advantage of a situation right away can't be taught. He just has it."

Crowds recognized that. Not surprisingly, home attendance his rookie season increased by 50 percent. On the road, the Cavs went from last in the league to first in attendance.

Recognition also came in the form of his being the youngest member of the 2004 US Olympic men's basketball team. That team stunningly lost, 92-73, in preliminary action to Puerto Rico in Athens, Greece, and finished the Summer Games with a disappointing bronze medal. It was the first time a US men's team had failed to win gold since professionals joined the roster. James spent most of the time on coach Larry Brown's bench and averaged just 5.8 points and 2.6 rebounds in 14.6 minutes per game.

Breaking Through to the Playoffs

At the start of his second season, James had only one thing on his mind: "I want to make the playoffs. That's my only goal."

He gave it a good try, improving in every significant statistical category and even leading the NBA in minutes per game (42.4). He played in 80 games, logged 25 double-doubles (double figures—10 or more—in two statistical categories), posted his first triple-double (27 points, 11 rebounds, 10 assists in a January 2005 win against the Portland Trail Blazers, one of four that year), ranked third in the league in scoring (27.2 points per game) and steals (2.2 per game), and sixth in assists (7.2 per game). He failed to score in double figures in only one game, scored 40 or more points five times, and became the youngest to score at least 50 points in a game with a 56-point outburst in a March 2005 loss to the Toronto Raptors. He accounted for 57 percent of his team's scoring in that loss.

But 2004–2005 was also a season during which James and coach Paul Silas did not see eye-to-eye much of the time. Tension was high as the team was fighting for a playoff spot. After leading their division early in the season, the Cavaliers slumped after the All-Star Break, dropping nine of twelve games and nine in a row on the road. Silas was fired in mid-March after the loss to Toronto, but the change did not come in time to save the season. The Cavs finished 42–40, out of the playoffs again.

The team hired a new coach, Mike Brown, for 2005–2006, and James really seemed to blossom, becoming the youngest player ever to score at least 30 points per game (31.4, third best in the league). He also won MVP honors at the 2006 All-Star Game, scoring twenty-nine points to help lead the East to a two-point victory, and finished runner-up to Phoenix Suns guard Steve Nash for MVP for the season. The team finished 50-32, the Cavs' best record since 1991–1992, and made the playoffs for the first time in eight seasons.

The Cavaliers won their first playoff game with James, who had 32 points, 11 rebounds, and 11 assists to help beat the Washington Wizards. He was the first player since Hall of Famer Magic Johnson in 1979-1980 to post a triple double in his NBA postseason debut. James missed repeating the feat in Game Two by one rebound. The best-of-seven series stood tied at 2-2, before James hit for 45 points and 32 points to help the Cavs win one-point overtime games to close out the Wizards, Cleveland's first postseason series victory since 1992–1993. James averaged 35.7 points, the most ever by a non-center in his playoff debut.

The excitement did not last long, however, as the Cavs lost the first two games of the next series against the Pistons in Detroit. Cleveland came back to win the next three, including a two-point victory in Game Five at Detroit in which James scored thirty-two points. But his shooting percentage was off, and the Pistons went on to win the series in seven games.

Remarkable Run

The only logical next step for James and the Cavaliers was making a serious run at the NBA championship, and 2006-2007 seemed the season, with the core of the team returning to action. The Cavs again finished 50-32, but dramatically improved at home, going from 19-22 the previous season to 30-11. James' averages were slightly down: 27.3 points, 6.7 rebounds and 6.0 assists. But with the number two seed in the Eastern Conference, and that .731 winning percentage at home, the Cavaliers were optimistic about their postseason chances.

The playoffs started well. They swept the Wizards in four games and took care of the Nets and Pistons in six games in each series to emerge as the Eastern Conference representatives in their first NBA Finals. The only problem: they had to defeat the veteran San Antonio Spurs, who were gunning for their fourth NBA championship in nine years under coach Gregg Popovich.

The Cavaliers had the big scoring superstar, but the Spurs had the team defense, with Tim Duncan in the middle, pesky guards in Tony Parker and Manu Ginobili, and the **stick-to-itiveness** of forward Bruce Bowen. The Spurs did their best to keep James from getting the ball or the opportunity to drive to the basket. That forced him to the outside, and his long-range shooting game was off. He averaged twenty-two points during the series but shot just 35.6

percent from the field (20 percent on three-point attempts), and made only 69 percent of his free throws.

Not too surprisingly, the Spurs breezed to opening home victories of nine points and eleven points before the series shifted to Cleveland. The games were much closer there, but the Spurs prevailed to end the Cavaliers' season in a sweep. "I have to be ten times better," James concluded immediately after the final game.

Driven to Succeed

James returned for the 2007–2008 season determined to fulfill that promise. He reached the 10,000 career points plateau just fifty-nine days after his twenty-third birthday, the youngest to achieve it. A few days after that, he passed Brad Daugherty as the franchise's all-time leading scorer. James ended the regular season averaging 30 points with 7.9 rebounds and 7.2 assists.

The Cavs, at 45–37, earned the number-four seed from the East in the playoffs. They again opened the playoffs by beating the Wizards but fell to the Boston Celtics in the conference semifinals in seven games.

Up next were the 2008 Summer Olympics in Beijing and a spot on the so-called "Redeem Team," which set the goal of winning the gold medal so the United States could reclaim its position as the premier basketball nation in the world. This time, James was a big part of the march to the gold medal, averaging 15.5 points, 5.3 rebounds and 3.8 assists as the team went undefeated. In the gold-medal game against Spain, James had fourteen points, seven rebounds, and three assists while shooting six–of–nine from the field.

James's first run with the Cavs ended in a 2010 playoff loss to the nemesis Boston Celtics. Here he drives against Tony Allen in the series finale.

Time Running Down in Cleveland

Back in Cleveland, the Cavaliers expected great things for the 2008–2009 season—and they carried through by **obliterating** their old record of fifty-seven wins, finishing with sixty-six, tops in the NBA and still a franchise record. In 81 games, James averaged 28.4 points, 7.6 rebounds and 7.2 assists. His shooting percentage, which had improved each season, was up to 48.9 percent (versus 41.7 percent as a rookie).

He was named to the All–Defensive First Team for the first time, to the All–NBA First Team for the second season in a row, and, finally, league Most Valuable Player.

"I never dreamed about being MVP, but if I said I didn't enjoy this award I'd be lying. Hard work pays off and dreams do come true," James said.

He asked to accept the award at St. Vincent-St. Mary. He arrived for the ceremony at the school after driving through his old neighborhoods—in a Ferrari with a police escort. Standing beneath the state championship banner from his 2003 senior season, James thanked his Cavaliers teammates and coaches by saying the award "is going to be like the both of ours, but I'm going to keep it at my house."

"He's never forgotten where he came from," his mother said at the ceremony. "I'm very proud of him. It is long overdue, and he's real deserving of it."

In the opening round of the 2009 playoffs, James averaged 32 points, 11.3 rebounds and 7.5 assists in a sweep of the Pistons. He backed that up in the next round by averaging 33.8 points, 8.3 rebounds, and 6.0 assists in a sweep of the Atlanta Hawks. It's hard to imagine, but he even topped those numbers in the Eastern Conference Finals against the Orlando Magic: 38.5 points, 8.3 rebounds, 8.0 assists. But the Magic had five players averaging in double figures, including dominating center Dwight Howard, and they outmuscled the Cavaliers to win in six games. When the series was over, James left the court without congratulating the Magic and was roundly criticized in the media.

Father Figure

As LeBron James's NBA career took off, people wanted to know more and more about the charismatic young man from Akron, Ohio. And in 2009, they got a chance to see James up close and personal during his high school days in the documentary *More Than a Game*. It was directed by Kristopher Belman, who originally shot film for what he believed would be a school project. The Akron native had gotten extraordinary access to the team from Coach Dru Joyce II, then realized as the years went by and James's popularity grew that he had enough for a feature-length film.

However, as Belman and James would discuss when the documentary came out, the real star of the film was Coach Dru, the coach/motivator/father figure James leaned on during his early years in basketball and throughout his media-crazy high school career.

"He not only helped us in basketball but helped us in life in general," James said.

Over the years when James slept at the Joyce's house, he became friends with Little Dru and experienced the sort of childhood many take for granted.

James wrote in the foreword to Coach Dru's book *Beyond Championships*: "On the court, the goal will always be to win a title. But off the court, the more important goal remains to shape the lives of young people in the community in the same way that Coach Dru shaped mine. And if I can do that, even just a little bit, then I will have accomplished something that means so much more to me than any championship."

Still trying to find the right combination around James, the Cavs brought in eventual Hall of Fame center Shaquille O'Neal for the 2009–2010 season. However, at thirty-seven, he was clearly on the downside of his career. James, at twenty-five, still had to shoulder the bulk of the offense and delivered again, averaging 29.7 points, 8.6 assists and 7.3 rebounds as the Cavaliers finished with the league's best record at 61–21. He also won the league MVP award in a landslide for the second season in a row.

The Cavaliers took care of the Chicago Bulls in five games in the first round of the playoffs before meeting their nemesis, the Celtics. James went into that series with an ailing right elbow—he had actually shot his final free throw of the Chicago series with his off (left) hand. The Cavs and Celtics split the opening four games. With the critical Game Five in Cleveland, the Cavs bombed, losing 120–88, with James scoring just 15 points and shooting 21.4 percent from the field. He perked up in Game Six at Boston, but his 27 points, 19 rebounds, 10 assists, and three steals were not enough. The team shot 38.4 percent from the field, committed 22 turnovers (including nine by James), and lost, 94–85.

James walked off the Celtics' celebrated **parquet** floor and was caught on camera in the players' tunnel tossing his jersey. Would he be wearing it again the next season?

Chapter 3

Leaving Home

After the 2009–2010 season, James became an unrestricted free agent, allowing him to negotiate to sign with any team. As the July 1 start to the signing period neared, it was all anyone could talk about: would he stay with the Cavaliers or play elsewhere? Every day presented a new rumor. Maybe he would be drawn to New York City, the Big Apple, and the Knicks. Maybe he would resurrect the winning ways of Jordan and take the Bulls back to a championship in Chicago.

Many thought it was a foregone conclusion he would leave, especially after All-Star guard Dwyane Wade signed to stay with the Miami Heat, where he had already won one NBA championship, and Toronto Raptors forward Chris Bosh, another unrestricted free agent, signed to join the Heat. South Beach certainly seemed a likely landing place for James. The three friends had set up their previous contracts to end at the same time, giving them the option to fulfill a dream and play together.

Opposite: LeBron James announces "The Decision" to leave the Cavaliers for the Miami Heat in a live, one-hour special on ESPN on July 8, 2010. He made the announcement before even informing the Cavaliers, for which he took a lot of criticism.

Still, for James in particular, the decision was not an easy one. He was the only one among the three with a hometown connection to consider. He would wake up one morning thinking he was off to another team, and the next day he would be considering staying, knowing what heartbreak he would bring to Cleveland, a city **derogatorily** referred to as the "Mistake by the Lake" for its proximity to Lake Erie and its longtime championship drought.

Representatives from many teams made their pitch to King James. Heat president Pat Riley let his championship rings do the talking: one as a player, one as an assistant, four as head coach of the Los Angeles Lakers, and one as head coach of the Heat. Playing for the Bulls, on the other hand, meant James would be staying close to his hometown of Akron and playing with a franchise full of winning tradition. Another contender, the New Jersey Nets, had a new owner willing to spend lots of money: Russian billionaire Mikhail Prokhorov. If it came down to money, the Cavaliers had the advantage of being able to offer the most to keep one of their own: a six-year deal worth roughly $125.5 million. Petitions in the Cleveland area were signed and circulated, begging James not to leave.

Not even the teams he was considering had a clue which way James was leaning. That did not stop the experts from weighing in. "It's fun to watch all the hoopla, but this is not a complex decision," said David Falk, Michael Jordan's longtime agent. "If I am LeBron, I have one question: Where can you win the most championships?"

"The Decision" to leave for Miami

To create some semblance of order from the media chaos, James said he would announce his decision on the evening of July 8 during a one-hour, prime-time, live interview conducted by reporter Jim Gray on ESPN. It was called "The Decision."

That night, James made the world wait almost until the end of the show. It was an agonizing decision, he said: "I think I decided this morning. I mean, I decided this morning. I went day to day. I wake up one morning, it's this team. I wake up another morning, it's this team. ... But this morning I woke up, had a great conversation with my mom. Once I had that conversation with her, I think I was set."

The major factor, he said, deciding it for him "was the best opportunity for me to win and to win now and to win into the future also. And winning is a huge thing for me. ... Ever since I was a rookie or even in high school ... that was the number one thing for me: Help my teammates get better and just wanting to win. And I've done some great things in my seven years, and I want to continue to do that."

And then it was time to reveal his choice:

> In this fall, this is very tough, in this fall I'm going to take my talents to South Beach and join the Miami Heat.

The overwhelmingly negative response that followed was unprecedented.

The **rancor** directed his way was a surprise to James, who could see on TV that Cavaliers fans were burning his jersey in bars and using them to build "bronfires" on the street. "For him to go on the air ... and stab us in the heart, he deserves everything he gets," Jason Heron, a local car salesman who started a bonfire, told ABC News at the time. "He's one of our own, that's what makes it so painful. ... LeBron can never come back."

Spurring the Decision

Of the factors that drove James to leave Cleveland, two stood out. One, he desperately wanted to play on a team with his friends, any combination of Chris Paul, Carmelo Anthony, or Dwyane Wade. Two, he could not get the Cavaliers over the hump against the Boston Celtics. His Cavaliers lost to the Celtics in seven games in the 2008 Eastern Conference semifinals and in six games in the 2010 conference semifinals.

In the 2008 series he averaged 26.7 points, 7.6 assists, 6.4 rebounds, 2.1 steals and 1.3 blocks— with 45 points in Game Seven. He accounted for 31 percent of the Cavaliers' scoring. The next highest scorer for the Cavs averaged just 11.9 points. The Celtics, meanwhile, were in their first season of the Big Three of Paul Pierce, Kevin Garnett, and Ray Allen, with a pesky Rajon Rondo thrown in for good measure. Those four shared the scoring load, combining for 70 percent of the Celtics' points, and wore down the Cavs.

In the 2010 series, James was even better, averaging 26.8 points, 9.3 rebounds, 7.2 assists, 2.2 steals, and 1.3 blocks. The Cavs even led the series two games to one— then lost the next three games in a collapse that would be James's final games in a Cleveland uniform until his return four years later.

The Game Six loss was particularly notable for a TV shot of James tossing his jersey on the way to the locker room.

"I thought that Boston team was prepared for us, was ready for us," James would say in recalling the

2010 series. "They beat us that series, and it stuck with me a lot."

Ultimately, he told *Business Insider* in August 2016, "It came down to me staying home or going to Miami once I knew that I needed to partner with some great players to get past Boston (to reach the NBA Finals). Boston was the team with Kevin Garnett and Ray Allen and Paul Pierce and Rajon Rondo. I knew that I had to get better with talent. And Dwyane Wade and Chris Bosh fit that mold."

LeBron James congratulates Kevin Garnett after losing a playoff series to Boston in six games in 2010.

FRIDAY, JULY 9, 2010

MAIN NEWS INSIDE

Gone.

*7 years
in Cleveland.
No rings.*

Reaction to LeBron James's decision to leave for Miami is swift and to the point, as in this July 9, 2010, front page to the (Cleveland) *Plain Dealer.*

Savannah Brinson, James's longtime girlfriend, later to become his wife, could not believe what she was seeing in the region she called home.

"You have fans, you think they're going to roll with you no matter what," she said in a 2010 interview with *Harper's Bazaar* magazine. "And then they burn your jersey? It's unfair. But they did it. It's over."

The Nasty Response

Helping to fuel the fire was the immediate, no-holds-barred reaction from Cavaliers owner Dan Gilbert, who was blindsided by the announcement. He posted a letter that night to the team's website, which in part read:

> I PERSONALLY GUARANTEE THAT THE CLEVELAND CAVALIERS WILL WIN AN NBA CHAMPIONSHIP BEFORE THE SELF-TITLED FORMER "KING" WINS ONE.
>
> You can take it to the bank. …

In a follow-up interview with the Associated Press, Gilbert went on to say that he believed James had quit on the team over his last two seasons with the Cavaliers.

For all those remarks and more, then-NBA Commissioner David Stern fined Gilbert $100,000 for a message he described as "a little bit extreme."

The Reverend Jesse Jackson, head of a Chicago-based civil rights group, said what Gilbert had done made James seem like a "runaway

Workmen begin taking down the building-sized advertisement featuring LeBron James after he left Cleveland.

slave." In a news release from his office, Jackson wrote: "He speaks as an owner of LeBron and not the owner of the Cleveland Cavaliers."

Reaction to James's announcement was swift from all corners. The huge Nike mural of James with his arms extended encompassing the side of a building near the Cavs' arena was torn down. Those fans who had not burned their Cavaliers jerseys with James's number 23 on them would wear them with a big "X" crossing out his name. Posters were stomped on. Some took to calling James "LeBum."

National reaction was largely negative, too. In New York, where the Knicks hoped James would land, the **vitriol** was almost as bad as in Cleveland. *Daily News* columnist Mitch Lawrence wrote: "He says he wants to win. But in making 'The Decision,' James basically threw up his hands and said, 'I give up. I can't lead a team to the title by myself.' And this guy thinks he can be another Michael Jordan?" *Washington Post* columnist Michael Wilbon wrote that James's decision "forbids LeBron from ever being one of those all-time greats who persevered through coaching changes, roster changes, and wrenching playoff losses." *Sports Illustrated* columnist Michael Rosenberg wrote that James "does not have the heart of a champion. He does not have the competitive fire of Jordan, the bull-headed determination of Kobe Bryant. … He is an extremely gifted player who wants the easy way out."

James took the words well. "I like criticism. It makes you strong," he said.

A Warm Welcome

Badly sent off from Cleveland, James was warmly welcomed in Miami, where the Heat threw a gigantic, in-your-face party at American Airlines Arena on July 9, 2010. Dwyane Wade, who had won the 2005-2006 NBA title with the Heat, and Chris Bosh, who chose to leave the Toronto Raptors after seven seasons for South Beach, joined James on stage to address the thunderous crowd of twelve thousand. It was the dawn of Miami's Big Three.

James said he came to the Heat to win "not one, not two, not three, not four, not five, not six, not seven" championships, much to the amusement of Wade and Bosh and the cheering crowd. "And when I say that I really believe it," James added. "I'm not just blowing smoke."

Miami's starting five for most of the 2010–2011 season was the Big Three plus center Zydrunas Ilgauskus and guard Carlos Arroyo.

The Decision got the opposite reaction in Miami to the one it did in Cleveland, as new teammates Dwyane Wade and Chris Bosh join LeBron James in a celebration of better times ahead for Heat fans.

Their coach was Erik Spoelstra, a former videotape procurer for the Heat, later an assistant coach to Pat Riley and just beginning his third season as the team's head coach. At forty, with not much head-coaching experience, Spoelstra was the center of much speculation as to whether he could command the respect of his new superstar and last even one season.

It did not help that Miami got off to a rocky start. In his first game with the Heat, playing his old nemesis the Celtics, James led all

LeBron James: King of the Court

scorers with thirty-one points, but Wade (thirteen points) was the only other teammate to score in double figures as Boston defeated Miami, 88–80. The Heat scored just nine points in their very first quarter together, shooting below 30 percent. Bosh finished with just eight points. James and Wade made fourteen turnovers combined.

"We all know Rome wasn't built in one day, so it's going to take time, and we understand that," James said.

But did they really? One month into the season, the Heat stood at 9–8 overall, losers of six of their last ten games. A 106–95 loss at the Dallas Mavericks prompted a players-only meeting, raising the decibel level on the rumors that Spoelstra's job was in jeopardy. It was during a third-quarter timeout in that game against the Mavericks that James and Spoelstra bumped into each other on the sideline. Was it intentional? Was someone trying to send a message?

Both men later met for thirty minutes and whatever happened seemed resolved by the next game, a 105–94 win at home against the Washington Wizards. James (thirty points), Wade (twenty-six), and Bosh (twenty) combined for seventy-plus points for the fourth time in the season. "I like it when we come in with a chip on our shoulder," Spoelstra said.

However, James and Wade hinted at the team's frustration. "We have to figure out how to complement each other on the court," said James. Said Wade: "Tonight is the second time (he and James) felt comfortable with each other taking over and not worrying about whether we are going to get a shot or get the ball."

There was scrutiny each and every time the Heat took the court, whether in practice or in a game. The media assigned to record their every move was extraordinary; the **idiom** "living in a fishbowl" never seemed more apt for the players.

Despite the attention, they rose to the challenge. The victory against the Wizards began a season-high twelve-game winning streak in which James averaged 26.1 points, 6.6 rebounds, and 6.3 assists and the team won by an average of 15.3 points. Over that stretch, James, Wade, and Bosh accounted for 70 percent of the Heat's scoring, including 75 points in an 89–77 win against the Atlanta Hawks.

Returning Home as the Opposition

What could top that for drama? How about James's initial return to Cleveland as a member of the Heat? It happened December 2, 2010, and James faced a **firestorm** of signs and boos, with obscenities yelled and fans chanting, "Akron hates you!" But his teammates rallied around him, and James scored a season-high thirty-eight points, including twenty-four in the third quarter, in a 118–90 blowout of the Cavs. James even sat out the entire fourth quarter.

"It's all right," James told TNT reporter Craig Sager at halftime. "I understand how passionate the fans are. I've got a lot of love for these fans, but I'm a Miami Heat player now looking to get this win."

Winning was what it was all about. The Big Three, good for at least 60 points and 20 rebounds most nights, led the Heat to a 58–24 record, an eleven-game improvement from the previous season, and to the number two seed in the Eastern Conference behind the Bulls. James led the team in points (26.7 per game), assists (7.0), and steals (1.6), and finished third in the MVP voting.

The NBA Finals was the target, and the Big Three took the Heat right there, losing a total of just three games in series victories against the Philadelphia 76ers, the Celtics, and the Bulls to set up a meeting with the Dallas Mavericks for the championship. The Heat

LeBron James scored a season-high thirty-eight points for the Heat in his first game back in Cleveland against the Cavaliers, here shooting over J.J. Hickson.

Leaving Home

split two close games at home and won the third game at Dallas, but the weight of expectations finally caught up with James. In Game Four he scored a season-low eight points, taking only eleven shots and making only three in an 86–83 loss.

"The fact that it happened in a loss is the anger part about it," James said. "That's all that matters to me."

He was only marginally better in the next two games, and the Mavericks took advantage to win their first NBA title.

"LeBron has been a lightning rod for a lot of everything, criticism and a lot of the noise that's been created outside," Spoelstra said after the final game. "I think it's really unfair. He made a tremendous sacrifice to come here, and he's been an ultimate team player."

Finally!

Lengthy negotiations for a new contract between the NBA and its players delayed the start of the 2011–2012 season until Christmas Day, when the Mavericks and Heat met up again in a nationally televised game from Dallas. A championship wasn't on the line, but James came ready to play, contributing 37 points, 10 rebounds, and 6 assists as the Heat won, 105–94. It would tip off a season in which Wade, the longtime Heat star, put the good of the team first and encouraged James to become its leader. And that he did, finishing third in the league in scoring (27.1 points per game) and fourth in steals (1.9), and continuing to improve his field goal shooting, raising it to a career-high 53.1 percent. The Heat benefited, cruising to a 46–20 record and the number two seed in the Eastern Conference behind the Bulls, and James was singled out again as the league MVP—his third such award in four seasons.

But he had a greater prize in mind—that elusive NBA championship. Once again, the Heat breezed through the early rounds of the playoffs, then faced the Celtics in the Eastern Conference finals. Boston was coming off a series against the Philadelphia 76ers that went the full seven games, and the Celtics players looked exhausted. The Heat won the opener in Miami by fourteen points, held off the Celtics to win Game Two, and looked in command of the series. However, as always for James, his matchups against the Celtics were never easy. The Celtics came alive at home, winning both games to tie the series, and then shocked the Heat by winning, 94–90, in Miami in Game Five.

The brunt of the criticism heaped on the Heat, as usual, was directed toward James, even though he had averaged 31.8 points through the first five games. On the brink of losing a shot at the title again, James took Game Six quite personally in the hostile environment of a raucous crowd at Boston's TD Garden. He put on what might have been his most brilliant performance to date, scoring forty-five points and grabbing fifteen rebounds in leading the Heat to a 98–79 victory that turned the series into a one-game showdown in Miami. It was the first time James had scored at least forty-five points in a Heat uniform, and he did it by making nineteen of twenty-six shots.

"I hope now you guys can stop talking about LeBron and that he doesn't play in big games," Celtics coach Doc Rivers said.

Rivers was witness to another big performance in Game Seven, as James combined thirty-one points with a dozen rebounds to close out the Celtics, 101–88. Boston actually led early in the fourth quarter, but a thunderous dunk by James and a three-pointer by Bosh gave Miami the lead for good and a second spot in a row in the NBA Finals. This time, the opponent was the Oklahoma City Thunder.

The Finals opened in Oklahoma City, and the Thunder won, 105–94, behind Kevin Durant's thirty-six points. James scored thirty points, but the whispers were starting again that he couldn't lead a team to a championship.

Four games later, those whispers had turned into roars of excitement. The Heat won by four points in Game Two to tie the series, then headed for three games in Miami. In Game Three, the Heat trailed by ten points midway through the third quarter but rallied to regain the lead at the end of the quarter on James's three-pointer. And when the Thunder seemed to come to life again, James scored five consecutive Miami points late in the fourth quarter to help build a lead the Heat would not surrender. But that was just a prelude to Games Four and Five, as James led the Heat in scoring, assists, and rebounds to clinch the championship and earn the NBA Finals MVP award.

It took a triple-double from James in Game Five to get it done—twenty-six points, thirteen assists, eleven rebounds—and end what Durant called "a storybook season for him."

"It's about damn time!" James said after accepting the MVP trophy, becoming the tenth player to win the regular-season and Finals MVP. "My dream has become a reality now, and it's the best feeling I ever had."

Wade, the teammate and close friend, basked in the enjoyment—and relief—James felt in achieving his dream: "I'm proud of him. He really took being the best player in the league to another level, and he did it all season long, man."

James had redefined his image. No longer could anyone say he couldn't win the big game. "It was a journey for myself," he told reporters. "All the ups and downs, everything that came along with it, I had to basically figure it out on my own. I'm happy now, nine years later since I've been drafted, that I can finally say that I'm a champion, and I did it the right way. I didn't shortcut anything. I put a lot of hard work and dedication in it, and hard work pays off."

Let's Win Two

The Heat played as well during the 2012–2013 season as nearly any team in history, reeling off 27 wins in a row in one stretch and finishing with a franchise-record 66 victories that still stands. James averaged 26.8 points, 8.0 rebounds, 7.3 assists, and 1.7 steals, shot 56.5 percent from the field and 40.6 percent from three-point range. MVP again? Of course, and just one vote shy of being a unanimous pick.

Miami cruised through playoff series against the Knicks and Bulls, losing just one game total, then needed seven games to dispose of the Indiana Pacers, with James averaging 29 points. That set up a finals matchup against the San Antonio Spurs, still led by coach Gregg Popovich, who had taken his team to victory against James and the Cavaliers in the 2007 NBA Finals. The Spurs had not won a title since but came into these Finals with a quality roster that included Tim Duncan, Tony Parker, Manu Ginobili, and Kawhi Leonard. The Heat had picked up a new cast member, too, in veteran guard Ray Allen, the career leader in three-point field goals made and attempted.

The Spurs raced out to a three-games-to-two series lead, with the final two games scheduled for Miami. They seemed to have Game Six under control and, with a three-point lead, were just 19.4 seconds from earning another NBA title. With time running down,

LeBron James reveled in holding the championship trophy a second year in a row, after the Heat beat the Spurs in the 2013 NBA Finals.

James missed a three-point shot from 26 feet (8 m) out. But Bosh grabbed the rebound and spotted Allen setting up in the corner. From 25 feet (7.6 m) out, with just 5.2 seconds left in regulation, Allen nailed the three-pointer to send the game into overtime. And with less than two minutes left in overtime, James sank a seven-footer for a one-point lead. The Heat held on for a 103–100 victory.

The championship came down to Game Seven, and James did not disappoint, scoring thirty-seven points—he made five three-pointers—and grabbing twelve rebounds as the Heat won, 95–88, to earn back-to-back NBA titles. James, who had eight points in the final five minutes and thirty-nine seconds, again was the Finals MVP.

"He's the best player I've ever seen in my life in person, hands down," Bosh said. "When we needed big shots, he hit them all. He hit them all."

As red and white confetti rained down on the champions at American Airlines Arena, James was as joyful as he had ever been.

"I can't worry about what everybody says about me," he said. "I'm LeBron James, from Akron, Ohio, from the inner city. I'm not even supposed to be here."

The Final Act in Miami

A month before the start of the 2013–2014 season, James and longtime sweetheart Savannah Brinson got married before two hundred guests at the Grand Del Mar resort in San Diego. James had proposed on New Year's Eve 2011. Performers Jay-Z and Beyoncé attended and sang "Crazy In Love" for the happy couple.

The season turned out crazy, too, with the media hyping the prospects of Miami becoming the first team to win three consecutive championships since the Los Angeles Lakers did it from 1999–2000 through 2001–2002. The Heat rolled to a 43–14 record, culminating on March 3, 2014, with James's career high of sixty-one points in a 124–107 win against the Charlotte Bobcats. But from that point until the end of the regular season, Miami went on a tailspin, winning just eleven of its final twenty-five games.

"It's the toughest season we've had since Year One just because of everything that comes with it," James told the *Palm Beach* (Florida) *Post.* "Just going out every night where you're the target and everyone gets up for you, and we have to find our own motivation every single night. It's not always about our opponent. It's about ourselves too."

However, James and the Heat stepped it up again in the playoffs, losing a total of just three games in series victories against the Bobcats, Brooklyn Nets, and Pacers. That set up, for the second year in a row, a meeting against the Spurs for the NBA title. The series began in San Antonio, and the teams split, with the next two games in Miami. The advantage should have gone to the Heat. But in Game Three, the Spurs jumped out to a 71–50 halftime lead, setting an NBA Finals record for field goal percentage in a half (75.8 percent). "They came out in a different gear than us," Spoelstra said after the eventual 111–92 loss.

Game Four was more of the same, as the Spurs made eleven of their first eighteen shots and extended their lead to 31–17 early in the second quarter. By halftime, the Heat trailed 55–36, and the outcome of the game was never really in doubt. The eventual 107–86 loss left Miami down three games to one in a series heading back to San Antonio. "Our heads are a little down right now," James said. "They smashed us two straight home games. ... It's that simple."

And it was that simple again in Game Five, a 104–87 Spurs' victory that gave San Antonio its fifth NBA championship under Popovich—and left James on the losing end of the NBA Finals for the third time in five tries. He did his best, pumping in thirty-one points, but Wade and Bosh combined for just twenty-five points, and the team shot 40 percent to San Antonio's 47.4 percent.

"It's been a hell of a ride these four years," Wade said. "When we decided to play together, we didn't say, 'OK, let's try for four years.' We said, let's just play together and let's see what happens. ... We'd love to be four-for-four (on titles). It just wasn't in the cards."

Now what was in the cards for the Big Three?

Chapter 4

Redemption

At twenty-nine, with the glamour of South Beach his for the taking, with two NBA titles and appearances in two other finals behind him, James could see a future that included becoming a Miami **icon**. He, Wade, and Bosh could all become free agents. They could set up shop with the Heat for the next few years and contend for more titles, although injuries and age were a concern about Wade, who was three years older than James, and Bosh at times could become ineffective during a game.

Those were not the key factors for James as he contemplated the next step of his career. His family had never really acclimated to Miami; Akron was still considered home. The way he had left Cleveland still tugged at him. The championship drought there had only grown, and neither the NFL's Browns nor MLB's Indians seemed ready to challenge any time soon. What would it mean to be the one who brought a title to Northeast Ohio? Could he imagine returning to the franchise and the city that rejected him so thoroughly when he left?

Opposite: As soon as LeBron James announced his return to the Cavaliers in June 2014, Cleveland businesses that had spurned him when he left rolled out the welcome-back signs.

Yes, he could. However, the timing for it to happen surprised even James.

"I had dreams about going back home, but I thought it would happen a lot later on in my career," he told CNN in 2014, "going back and kind of having a couple more years left in my career and kind of finishing it off that way. But I didn't think it would happen this soon."

His family—including sons LeBron Jr. and Bryce Maximus—was the main factor in **hastening** his return to Ohio. (His daughter, Zhuri, was born October 22, 2014, a week before James's first game back with the Cavs.) While James was playing in Miami, his wife mainly had stayed in Akron raising the kids.

"As a kid, I didn't have much money. It was just my mom and me, and things were rough at times," James recalled in an editorial for *Business Insider* in October 2016. "But I had basketball. That gave me a family, a community, and an education. That's more than a lot of children in Akron can say. There are a lot of people who want to tell kids who grew up like me and looked like me that they just don't have anything to look forward to. That's dead wrong. And that's why I came back to Cleveland, to continue my second mission. … Opportunities, a support system, and a safety net for kids in poverty or kids in single-parent households shouldn't be limited to those lucky enough to be blessed with athletic talent."

James made his announcement in a letter published by *Sports Illustrated* on June 11, 2014.

> My relationship with Northeast Ohio is bigger than basketball. I didn't realize that four years ago. I do now. …

I feel my calling here goes above basketball. I have a responsibility to lead, in more ways than one, and I take that very seriously. My presence can make a difference in Miami, but I think it can mean more where I'm from. I want kids in Northeast Ohio, like the hundreds of Akron third-graders I sponsor through my foundation, to realize that there's no better place to grow up. Maybe some of them will come home after college and start a family or open a business. That would make me smile. Our community, which has struggled so much, needs all the talent it can get.

In Northeast Ohio, nothing is given. Everything is earned. You work for what you have.

I'm ready to accept the challenge. I'm coming home.

Heat president Pat Riley took the news hard, although better than Cavaliers owner Dan Gilbert did when James left for Miami.

"I don't want to go back in history, but after forty-five years [in basketball], I think I've been around at least fifteen **transcendent** players that have walked out the door—either left the team, retired, got traded, went somewhere else, and you move on," Riley told reporters in July 2014. "We were shocked (by James's departure), but we recovered. People in this country have the right to do what they want to do. He wanted to go home. In our statements, we respected that. It was a tough blow."

You can go home again

James, who signed a two-year, $42 million contract, looked past what Gilbert had said about him when he left the franchise in 2010; that's how strong his love for Northeast Ohio was. Gilbert had written that James's decision to leave Cleveland for Miami was "cowardly" and **derided** him by mocking one of the player's nicknames and calling him the "chosen one."

How does someone forgive that?

"I'm a man. Men, we all make mistakes," James said in an interview with ESPN at the time. "As a man, if you got a problem with somebody, you sit down face-to-face and you talk to them eye-to-eye. And you hash it out and move on. So, I think a lot of things that go on in life or in sports with people kind of holding grudges is because they're afraid to actually take a step forward. It's a fine line between pride and progress, and I'm on the progress side. I'm not on the pride side."

Even the car salesman in Akron who said James could never come home had to eat his words. "I said a lot of things I regret," Jason Herron told reporters.

Cavs owner Dan Gilbert acknowledged some regrets, too, saying of James, "We had five great years (together) and one bad night," when the player announced his departure from Cleveland on live TV before informing the team.

That mural of James that had been immediately taken down after he announced he was leaving Cleveland for Miami? As the season opener to James's second act in Cleveland neared, workmen were finishing hanging a 10-story Nike banner with James's likeness on a building downtown.

Fan reaction was so intense that the price for tickets to home games on the secondary market—people selling their seats to individual games—rose 224 percent, to an average of $388, more expensive than for any team in the league. According to CNBC, those tickets for opening night averaged $588, with a front-row ticket to James's return costing nearly $14,000 on online ticket marketplace StubHub. The economic boost for Cleveland and Cuyahoga County was estimated at $50 million, from more jobs being created to meet greater tourist interest and more taxes collected from increased consumer spending.

During James's four years away from the Cavs, the team had lost more games than any NBA franchise, and a championship in his first season back seemed unlikely. The team had a spectacular but young guard in Kyrie Irving, who in three seasons was averaging 20.7 points and shooting almost 45 percent from the field. However, Irving was also hampered by injuries that kept him sidelined a great deal for a player only twenty-two years old. The Cavaliers also had landed a strong rebounder in free agent Kevin Love, who came to the Cavaliers after a spectacular six initial years in the NBA with the Minnesota Timberwolves. Love was averaging 19.2 points and 12.2 rebounds and, for a six foot ten inch (2.1 m), 251-pound (114 kilogram) inside player, could pop in jumpers from mid-range and even three-point range from the corners.

So the makings of a good team were there for James, although hardly the formula to an automatic title—which everyone was expecting. Only five of the fifteen players from the previous season's 33–49 team were back. The coach was not only new, but a first-time NBA head coach; David Blatt had been a standout in Europe as the winning coach of Maccabi Tel Aviv, the Russian national team, and various Turkish teams. However, this was the NBA, not Turkey. Blatt had been signed before it was known James would be returning. Speculation was **rife** on how long this coach would last. That was all in the future. For the present, James knew the situation he was facing.

It helped the Cavaliers that the balance of power in the league had shifted to the Western Conference, where the San Antonio Spurs, Golden State Warriors, Dallas Mavericks, and others could wear each other out before getting to the NBA Finals. In the East, the Boston Celtics were in decline, the Chicago Bulls could not rely on an oft-injured Derrick Rose, and the Indiana Pacers couldn't sustain momentum through playoff series after playoff series.

"One of the Biggest Sporting Events"

With that as the backdrop, James took the floor in his first regular-season game at Quicken Loans Arena in his second go-round as a Cavalier—and the crowd went crazy as the arena darkened and the image of James appeared on the massive new HD scoreboard screens, said to be the largest anywhere with "5,550 total square feet of LED technology." As he stared out at the fans from the Humongotron, which is what the Cavaliers call the scoreboard, James proclaimed, "There's no place like home!" Earlier, in the pregame session with the media, James was asked how big this game was for him in the totality of his career. "This is probably one of the biggest sporting events that is up there ever," he said plainly.

You think? Usher sang the national anthem, and celebrities sighted included singer Justin Bieber, NFL great Michael Strahan, and then-Cleveland Browns quarterback Johnny Manziel. Just before tipoff, James punctuated the moment with his famous pregame

Before the start of his first home game back as a Cavalier on Oct. 30, 2014, LeBron James sprayed the crowd with his hand-clapping chalk toss.

Redemption

ritual—95 percent of fans had who responded to a question posted by James on Twitter voted for him to do this: He stepped up to the scorer's table and sprayed the crowd with the particles from his hand-clapping chalk toss. Indeed, every fan in attendance had been given packets of talcum powder to commemorate the occasion.

Then the team went out and bombed. Carmelo Anthony scored twenty-five points and the New York Knicks shot 53.6 percent from the field in a 95–90 victory over the Cavs. James made just five of fifteen shots from the field for seventeen points, and he committed eight turnovers. Was it nerves? "I didn't press. I didn't do much," he said. "It was a special night … but I'm also glad it's over."

A Championship Run?

It took a while for James, Irving, and Love to blend their talents—the Heat, after all, had gone 9–8 to open their first season with James, Wade, and Bosh together—and injuries kept James sidelined for a couple of weeks in late December and early January. Then the Cavs went on a second-half tear, winning thirty-four of forty-three games to finish the season with fifty-three victories, good for the number-two seed in the East but still seven games behind the number-one-seeded Atlanta Hawks.

Come playoff time, Cleveland's chances looked good, but then things began to unravel. In the final game of a sweep of the Celtics, Love dislocated his shoulder when he and Boston's Kelly Olynyk were going for the ball and Olynyk seemed to clamp down on and pull Love's left arm. Love would be out for the rest of the playoffs. The Cavs got past the Bulls in six games and swept the Hawks in the conference finals. However, Irving was dealing with tendinitis in his

LeBron James was matter-of-fact about the injury-depleted Cavaliers losing to the Golden State Warriors in the 2015 NBA Finals. He did his part, averaging 35.8 points, 13.3 rebounds and 8.8 assists in the six-game series.

left knee, putting his role in the NBA Finals against the Golden State Warriors in doubt.

Indeed, with two minutes left in overtime of Game One, Irving reinjured the knee driving against the Warriors' Klay Thompson. He fell to the floor, grimacing, and left Golden State's Oracle Arena on crutches. James scored forty-four points but needed to take thirty-eight shots to get them, and he missed on a fallaway jumper being defended by Golden State's Andre Iguodala at the end of regulation that might have won the game for Cleveland. Instead, the Warriors prevailed in overtime to go ahead, one game to none, in the Finals. "At the end of the day we gave ourselves a chance," James said. "I missed a tough one. But we had so many opportunities to win this game, but we didn't."

They would not have Irving for the rest of the Finals—he had fractured his left kneecap and required surgery. That left basically James alone against the hot-shooting Warriors. In the eventual six-game series, he averaged 35.8 points, 13.3 rebounds and 8.8 assists, and it wasn't enough to stop the Warriors from winning their first NBA title in 40 years. "We ran out of talent," James said after the final game. "If I could've [given] more, I would've done it."

Is this the season?

As luck would have it, after splitting two road games to open the 2015–2016 season, the Cavs played their first home game against the Miami Heat. James made thirteen of twenty-nine shots, scoring twenty-nine points in the 102–92 victory. Love was back, adding twenty-four points and fourteen rebounds, but Irving would not return to the lineup until the twenty-fifth game of the season. By then, the Cavs had romped to a 17–7 record and were in the midst of an eventual six-game winning streak. Irving scored twelve points in his return, a 108–86 victory against the Philadelphia 76ers.

By January 22, 2016, the Cavaliers were rolling along with an Eastern Conference-leading 30–11 record, with James scoring thirty or more points in ten games, and seemed headed for another shot at reaching the NBA Finals. So when Cavs general manager David Griffin fired Coach Blatt and replaced him with assistant coach and former NBA guard Tyronn Lue, the head-scratching observers naturally turned to what role James had had in the decision.

"What I see is that we need to build a collective spirit, a strength of spirit, a collective will," Griffin said. "Elite teams always have that, and you see it everywhere. To be truly elite, we have to buy into a set of values and principles that we believe in. That becomes our identity. … I have never seen a locker room not be as connected after wins as they need to be. We've only been galvanized when expectations were not high."

Griffin said he did not talk to any of the players before his decision, but that did not stop the speculation around James, who denied any involvement but agreed team chemistry was an issue: "We're a team that gets fragile at times, and we're still learning each other. … Guys don't know how to figure it out together. So hopefully we can kind of right the ship and be better for one another before we even talk about the game."

The Cavaliers lost their first game with Lue as coach but finished out the season on a 27–14 run and earned the number one playoff seed in the Eastern Conference. They swept the Detroit Pistons and Atlanta Hawks and took care of the Toronto Raptors in six games to reach the NBA Finals—again against the Golden State Warriors,

LeBron James was overcome with emotion after leading the Cavaliers to victory in Game Seven of the 2016 NBA Finals against the Warriors, the first sports title for the city of Cleveland in more than fifty years.

who not only had the best record in the league but had set the all-time mark for victories with seventy-three.

This time it was the Warriors who were hurting, especially their star guard—three-point shooting whiz and back-to-back league MVP Stephen Curry. However, that did not stop them from grabbing a three-games-to-one series lead, and the games were not even close. In the 108–97 victory at Cleveland's Quicken Loans Arena in Game Four, Curry finished with thirty-eight points, and the Warriors set a Finals record by hitting seventeen three-pointers—this despite James and Irving combining for fifty-seven points and both playing the entire second half. The game also was marked by a flagrant foul called on Golden State's Draymond Green, who got tangled with James. Green fell to the floor, and after James stepped over him to walk away, Green swung his arm and appeared to hit James in the groin. The two then had to be separated. It was costly for the Warriors, as Green was suspended for Game Five.

However, the Warriors felt confident with the series going back to Oakland. No team had ever come back from a 3–1 deficit in thirty-two such situations to win in the NBA Finals. Coach Lue was adamant his team would be ready. "If you don't think you can win," he told the players, "don't get on the plane."

The players took that to heart. They fell behind early in Game Five, but tied the score by halftime. In the third quarter, James and Irving each scored eleven points, and the team defense in the fourth quarter held the Warriors to just thirteen points as the Cavs won, 112–97. James and Irving each finished with forty-one points, becoming the first teammates to score forty or more points in a Finals game.

"Whatever it takes to win," Irving said. "We're not satisfied. We understand what the magnitude of Game Six means to us at home."

Back in Cleveland, the Cavaliers jumped out to an 8–0 lead, led by twenty points after the first quarter, and were never seriously threatened in a 115–101 victory. James poured in another forty-one points, including eighteen in a row (two with a spectacular alley-oop dunk) in one stretch of the second half. The series was down to a winner-take-all final in Oakland. "It's two of the greatest words in the world, and that's 'Game Seven,' so I'll play it anywhere," James said.

Three guesses how Game Seven turned out. Not that it wasn't close. James didn't turn on the juice until the second half, but when he did, it was lights out for the Warriors. He made a highlight reel chase-down block of Andre Iguodala with the game on the line, Irving sank a long three-pointer to break an 89–89 tie, and James sealed it with a free throw for a 93–89 championship victory. James finished with twenty-seven points, eleven rebounds, and eleven assists, led both teams for the series in points, rebounds, assists, blocks, and steals, and was named the Finals MVP.

Championship Quotes

I came back to bring a championship to our city. I knew what I was capable of doing. I knew what I learned in the last couple years that I was gone, and when I came back, I knew I had the right ingredients and the right blueprint to help this franchise get back to a place that we've never been. That's what it was all about." —LeBron James

"I watched Beethoven tonight." —Teammate Kyrie Irving of James's performance in the Game Seven win for the NBA title against the Warriors

"He stared all of the doubters in the face, including myself, and made his presence felt." —Actor and basketball fan Kevin Hart on the Cavaliers' championship

"It was pandemonium. There was definitely no crying. There was so much laughter and joking and excitement. Our franchise took us to Vegas from San Francisco (after the title win). Guys partied there, and then we went home and had another celebration. So we had a five-hour flight back to Cleveland in front of our fans, and they were there waiting at the airport. No one slept. We were so high off adrenaline and emotions and everything." —LeBron James

"When he came back, there was so much talk about not one, can he get us two (titles), can we make it a dynasty? Now that it's happened, nothing else matters. (Leaving for) Miami doesn't matter. Cleveland was validated with the (NBA title) win." —Radio host Nick Wilson, Cleveland's 92.3 The Fan

"There's no doubt who the best player in the world is. Period. It's LeBron James, and it might stay that way for a while longer." —AP basketball writer Tim Reynolds

Fans in Ohio were in full celebration mode as the 2016 NBA champion Cavaliers arrived at the airport in Cleveland.

"For us to be able to end this drought, our fans deserve it. They deserve it," he said.

"Just knowing what our city has been through, Northeast Ohio has been through, as far as our sports and everything for the last fifty-plus years," James said of how special this championship was. "Our fans, they ride or die, no matter what's been going on, no matter the Browns, the Indians, the Cavs and so on, and all other sports teams. They continue to support us. And for us to be able to end this, end this drought, our fans deserve it. They deserve it. And it was for them."

And maybe just a little vindication for himself.

"Throughout my thirteen-year career," James said, "I've done nothing but be true to the game, give everything I've got to the game, put my heart, my blood, sweat, tears into the game, and people still want to doubt what I'm capable of doing. So that was a little icing on the cake for myself to just let me know that everything I've done, it results in this. They say hard work pays off, and that's what happened tonight."

Chapter 5

More Than Just Basketball

He's not an icon like Michael Jordan, who won six NBA titles and created a brand that is not just known all over the world but valued as well.

Not yet.

"My career is totally different than Michael Jordan's," James told *Sports Illustrated* in the summer of 2016. "What I've gone through is totally different than what he went through. What he did was unbelievable, and I watched it unfold. I looked up to him so much. I think it's cool to put myself in position to be one of those great players, but if I can ever put myself in position to be the greatest player, that would be something extraordinary."

He is already seen as extraordinary in his hometown.

The LeBron James Family Foundation

The Akron community remains close to James's heart. About the city, he once posted to his Facebook page: "It's like my father, it's

Opposite: It was a joyous ride for LeBron James and the Cavaliers as they rolled through downtown Cleveland in a championship parade on June 22, 2016.

Family means the world to James, who grew up without a father and has done much to improve life for disadvantaged youth.

like my brother, it's like my mother, it's like my grandmother, it's like everything to me."

He wrote about Akron in his book *Shooting Stars*, giving credit to a community of "people taking care of things, people taking care of each other, people who found you and protected you and treated you like their own son even when you weren't."

Among his good works: The announcement in September 2016 of a donation of green, gold, and white Nike jerseys and shorts to the cross-country and track-and-field teams at Akron's Firestone High School through the LeBron James Family Foundation.

"Uniforms are nice, but the message is more relevant and **resonates**," principal Larry Johnson told the *Akron Beacon Journal*. "Strive for greatness, make sure you're exhibiting good sportsmanship on and off the floor, and make sure you're a model student–athlete to your community is what LeBron James always talks about."

That is the message on the website of James's foundation: "Going to school is to you guys what going to practice is for me. We can only get better if we practice and work our hardest."

Another recent venture with his foundation: partnering with the University of Akron to provide college scholarships to students who can keep at least a 3.0 grade-point average.

"We have a promise initiative, where the kids promise me they will go to school, that they'll listen to their teachers, that they'll be great to their classmates," James told *Business Insider* in August 2016. "And I promise them that I will continue to be a great role model, a father figure for them, and not let those guys down."

By 2016, he had committed $41 million to his foundation's Akron I Promise program. But that's not all. In helping families toward college scholarships for their children, James and the foundation realized that many of the parents had not completed high school themselves.

"So not only are we tracking our kids here to make them become better, we're also lending a helping hand to a lot of the parents that didn't graduate high school, and putting them in programs where they can get their high school diploma, and get a GED," James said in a 2016 interview with ESPN.

Being there for his family is a priority for James, particularly given how his father was not there for him. In the aftermath of the Cavaliers' first NBA championship, James wanted to be sure three photos were taken: one with his mother, one with his close friends from childhood, and one with his wife and their three children. All coming on Father's Day. He recognized how family puts everything in perspective.

"I wanted to be a part of the statistics that breaks the mode of fathers running out on their kids. That was something that I obviously went through and I knew from Day One that wasn't going to be me," he told Cleveland.com. "So, to have a family and be there for them and be there on a day-to-day basis is important. I know I travel a lot but I'm a **staple** in the household and it means a lot to me and I know it means a lot to my kids."

Social activism

Former NBA star and current broadcaster Charles Barkley famously said, "I'm not a role model," but James views his position differently.

"Once you become a professional athlete or once you do anything well, then you're automatically a role model. … I have no problem being a role model. I love it. I have kids looking up to me and hopefully I inspire these kids to do good things," James said.

In addition to his work with the foundation, James has not been afraid to speak out publicly on issues of the day, particularly violence against youth.

His voice was perhaps the loudest among athletes over the 2012 fatal shooting of unarmed seventeen-year-old Trayvon Martin during an altercation in Florida with a male neighborhood watch volunteer. James and his Miami Heat teammates wore hooded sweatshirts, similar to what Martin was wearing when he was killed, and bowed their heads before a March game against the Detroit Pistons. James also tweeted a photo of the message he wrote on the tip of his sneakers—"RIP Trayvon Martin"—and arranged a team photo of the players in the hooded sweatshirts.

"It was very emotional, an emotional day for all of us," James said then. "Taking that picture, we're happy that we're able to shed light on the situation that we feel is unjust."

It would not be the last time James got involved. During the 2014 season, James and teammate Kyrie Irving wore "I Can't Breathe" T-shirts while warming up for a game in Brooklyn, New York, after a Staten Island grand jury's decision not to **indict** a police officer in the choking death of an unarmed black male. James also spoke out in November 2014 following a grand jury decision in Ferguson, Missouri not to indict a police officer for the shooting of an unarmed black teen. In October 2015, he called for stronger gun laws after the fatal shooting of a five-month-old in Cleveland.

"This is our country, the land of the free, and we keep having these incidents happen, innocent victims or whatever the case may be," James told Cleveland.com in December 2015. "Our families are losing loved ones. I'm not pointing the blame at anybody that's making it happen. In society, we've come a long way, but it just goes to show how much further we still have to go."

James joined the chorus of athletes in 2016 who expressed support for the **Black Lives Matter** movement. Perhaps the most

After unarmed teenager Trayvon Martin was killed in 2012 in Sanford, Florida, LeBron James, then with the Heat, wrote a message on the tip of his sneakers in outrage.

LeBron James: King of the Court

striking example came at the 2016 ESPY awards, where NBA superstars James, Dwyane Wade, Chris Paul, and Carmelo Anthony began the show by speaking out against that summer's wave of police shootings of black men and subsequent revenge shootings of law enforcement officers. James was the last to speak:

> We all feel helpless and frustrated by the violence. We do. But that's not acceptable. It's time to look in the mirror and ask ourselves, "What are we doing to create change?" I know tonight we'll honor Muhammad Ali. … To do his legacy any justice, let's use this moment as a call to action to all professional athletes to educate ourselves, explore these issues, speak up, use our influence, and renounce all violence. And most importantly go back to our communities. Invest our time, our resources. Help rebuild them. Help strengthen them. Help change them. We all have to do better. Thank you.

The speeches that July night were recalled later in the summer when fatal shootings of unarmed black men by police continued. **Emboldened** by the leadership of James et al. at the ESPYs, the NBA and the National Basketball Players Association sent a memo to all players announcing their joint venture to begin "developing substantive ways for us to come together and take meaningful action. … (The four stars) spoke eloquently about the senseless acts of violence impacting our communities."

James chose to honor Muhammad Ali himself by donating, along with his foundation and business partner Maverick Carter, $2.5 million to support an exhibit on the late heavyweight champion at the new Smithsonian Museum of African American History and Culture in Washington, DC. The exhibit is titled "Muhammad Ali: A Force for Change." Among the other major celebrity donors are Michael Jordan and Magic Johnson and his wife Cookie.

The sentiments expressed in his speech were one reason James decided to endorse Hillary Clinton in her failed run for president in 2016. "Only one person running truly understands the struggles of an Akron child born into poverty," James wrote in an editorial in support of Clinton published in October 2016 by *Business Insider*. "We must address the violence, of every kind, the African-American community is experiencing in our streets and seeing on our TVs. … However, I am not a politician, I don't know everything it will take finally to end the violence. But I do know we need a president who brings us together and keeps us unified."

After the election, James posted a message of hope on Instagram: "Parents and leaders of our children, please let them know they can still change the world for the better. Don't lose a bit of faith! They're our future and we must remain stronger than ever!!"

On to the Next Season

Before the start of the 2016–2017 NBA season in defense of the Cavaliers' title, James remained just as motivated, just as prepared to put in the work to achieve the level of greatness he seeks. Another set of back-to-back titles would help.

"My hometown team, I can't be more excited in this opportunity to defend our crown," James said in a video posted to the website he has created as a vehicle for athletes to express themselves, aptly named Uninterrupted. "It was an unbelievable season, and I just can't wait to get the group back together."

And he's not satisfied. Remember, that is not an option for him.

"We're not satisfied," James told reporters at the team's practice facility before training camp opened. "We're not satisfied with just winning one championship. We're not satisfied with just being successful. We want to continue to get better."

That would help explain why his workout routine remains as impressive as ever; he wakes up at 5 a.m. to get started. "My workout **regimen** is pretty much five times a week, every day. And it varies," James told *Business Insider* in August 2016. "Sometimes I stay at home and work out. Sometimes I'll go to an actual class. I've been to, like, **VersaClimber** classes, or spinning classes. I do Pilates as well. So, it kind of varies depending on how I'm feeling."

The glow of the championship spread all over Cleveland that summer, and into the fall as the Cavaliers prepared to begin defense of their title. As training camp opened, the team could not escape questions from the media about what the experience meant to them. Player after player would say they repeatedly had rewound the tape and watched again, to make sure it really had happened.

"I've seen it a few times," James told reporters. "It was on NBA TV throughout the summer. I watch it from a fan's perspective. I see what we could've done better, but I also watch it for enjoyment, to see those three zeros on the clock" as time ran out on the Warriors.

To open the 2016–2017 season, on the night they received their rings and the NBA championship banner was raised to the rafters of Quicken Loans Arena, the Cavaliers tipped off against the New York Knicks, one of the teams James once considered joining. Naturally, he registered a triple-double. The NBA Finals rematch would come Christmas Day, with the Warriors playing in Cleveland.

Then it was time to turn his attention to defending the title. "I always look forward. I try not to dwell in the past," James said. "There are going to be so many challenges for us. We have to be mentally focused. And we will."

Hollywood–Bound

With the retirements of certain Hall of Famers Kobe Bryant and Tim Duncan after the 2015–2016 season, James and his 2003 draft class buddies are among the highest profile stars in the game.

"It feels like our era is next," James said. "You just don't take it for granted. … We're going to play this game—we love it—but we're on deck."

James has already been preparing for the day when playing basketball is no longer his job. He is, for instance, no stranger to Hollywood and entertainment and is scheduled to star in the upcoming remake of Michael Jordan's *Space Jam*, in partnership with Warner Bros.

"Michael Jordan and the Looney Tunes—they did an unbelievable thing not only for my childhood, but for so many kids and so many people that followed the franchise," James told *Business Insider* in August 2016. "So, obviously, we want to make sure that it's right. We don't want to rush it. We don't want to do something that's not authentic to the *Space Jam* brand."

He already has appeared on such TV series as *Entourage*, *The Simpsons*, and *SpongeBob SquarePants*. His production company has a comedy show on Starz, *Survivor's Remorse*, and a reality show on CNBC, *Cleveland Hustles*, which gives the average person with a

Amy Schumer was the star of the 2015 film *Trainwreck*, but LeBron James stole the show.

dream to start a company a chance to make that dream come true. A game show also is coming soon to NBC. He has done commercials for Nike, Sprite, McDonald's, Kia, Verizon, and Beats.

James and his manager, childhood friend Maverick Carter, also created a website, Uninterrupted, which provides a multimedia platform for athletes to "provide **uncensored**, real-time perspectives on the topics they most want to address," as *Bleacher Report* described what are essentially video testimonials from players.

Warner Bros. and Turner Sports have invested $15.8 million in Uninterrupted, which James described in a news release "as a place for athletes to go to connect with fans and share their stories in a different way."

All told, James earned $77 million in 2016 from salary and endorsements. Only two athletes made more, and both play the world's most popular sport, soccer: Cristiano Ronaldo and Lionel Messi.

"You know, God gave me a gift to do other things besides play the game of basketball," James has said.

One of his most recent ventures is working with NBC to develop three shows: a game show, a half-hour sitcom, and an hour-long drama. The one-hour game show, *The Wall*, is where everyday people "can achieve their dreams with one bounce of the ball." The comedy, *There Goes the Neighborhood*, is about a white family moving into a predominantly black Cleveland neighborhood. The drama is about "a brilliant doctor, specializing in treating the world's greatest sports stars, [who] undergoes a health crisis that forces him to rethink his approach to medicine with the help of a gifted sports psychologist."

The latter would be a logical next step after James's role in the 2015 big-screen hit *Trainwreck*, playing a high-profile athlete who befriends a talented surgeon with many top sports stars as his patients.

Celebrities seem to be lining up to do projects with James. Actor Mark Wahlberg, during a guest appearance in September 2016 on *The Tonight Show Starring Jimmy Fallon*, said he would love to do a movie with James based around a fantasy league: "It's actually a great idea. These guys get to go to one of these fantasy camps, and me and LeBron have a 'situation.' "

LeBron James Scorecard

Career Highlights: Three-time NBA champion (2011–12, 2012–13, 2015–16); All-NBA First Team ten times (2006, 2008–2016); All-Defensive NBA First Team five times (2009–2013);

Four-time regular season MVP (2009, 2010, 2012, 2013); three-time NBA Finals MVP (2012, 2013, 2016); two-time All-Star MVP (2006, 2008); league scoring champion, 2008 (30.0 ppg); twelve-time All-Star (2005–2016).

Firsts: Drafted number one overall by the Cleveland Cavaliers on June 26, 2003; 2004 Rookie of the Year, youngest ever; youngest/fastest to 10,000 points, 2,500 rebounds, 2,500 assists, 700 steals and 300 blocks, Nov. 3, 2008; 2016–17 salary, $31 million, tops in the NBA; first in minutes per game among active players (he's second in points, field goals, and free throw attempts, and third in assists and steals).

Honors: Ohio Mr. Basketball (2001–2003); *Sports Illustrated* Sportsman of the Year (2012); *Sporting News* Athlete of the Year (2012); Associated Press Male Athlete of the Year (2013); ESPY awards: Best male athlete (2006, 2009, 2010, 2012–2016); best NBA player (2005–2016); best breakthrough athlete (2013–2014); Greater Cleveland Sports Commission Professional Athlete of the Year, (2004–2006, 2009, 2015), and High School Athlete of the Year, (2001–2002); Greater Akron Chamber of Commerce H. Peter Burg Award, (March 2015).

Knowing Hollywood celebrities is one of the **perks** that comes with fame. So is living in style. In Akron, James owns a seven-plus acre property that includes a 30,000-square-foot (2,878 square meters) mansion with six bedrooms and fourteen bathrooms. After leaving the Heat, James sold his Coconut Grove, Florida, waterfront property for a reported $13.4 million. *Variety* reported in November 2015 that James laid out $21 million for a 9,350-square-foot (869 sq m) mansion in the trendy Brentwood section of Los Angeles that included six bedrooms and seven bathrooms.

To celebrate his wife's thirtieth birthday in 2016, James surprised her with a red bow-tied Ferrari Testarossa—the car made famous on the 1980s TV series *Miami Vice.*

Looking Ahead

James signed a contract extension during the summer of 2016. By the end of that extension, which was to last through the 2017–2018 season, he would be approaching his thirty-fourth birthday. That's young in life but getting up there in basketball years.

That is why James has his hands into so many things beyond his playing career—including the thought of one day owning a franchise.

"I feel like my brain as far as the game of basketball is unique, and I would love to continue to give my knowledge to the game," James said during an appearance on the "Open Run" podcast in August 2016. "And I would love to be a part of a franchise, if not at the top. My dream is to actually own a team, and I don't need to have fully hands on. If I'm fortunate enough to own a team, then I'm going to hire the best GM and president that I can. But I have a feel, like I have a good eye for not only talent, because we all see a lot of talent, but the things that make the talent, the chemistry, what type of guy he is, his work ethic, his passion, the basketball IQ side of things, because talent only goes so far."

He experienced all that with the Cavaliers' 2016 journey to the NBA title. "That moment will never be forgotten," James said. "It will go down in history."

Timeline

December 30, 1984: LeBron Raymone James is born in Akron, Ohio.

March 24, 2001: Scores twenty-five points and grabs ten rebounds to pace St. Vincent-St. Mary to the Ohio state championship.

March 22, 2003: Scores twenty-five points and pulls down eleven rebounds to lead St. Vincent-St. Mary to a third Ohio state title.

June 26, 2003: Chosen first overall by the Cleveland Cavaliers in the NBA draft.

April 20, 2004: Named NBA Rookie of the Year, youngest ever at nineteen, averaging 20.9 points, 5.9 assists, 5.5 rebounds.

June 14, 2007: Cavs are swept by the San Antonio Spurs in the NBA Finals.

May 4, 2009: Wins first NBA MVP award, averaging 28.4 points, 7.6 rebounds, 7.2 assists.

May 13, 2010: Totals twenty-seven points, nineteen rebounds, and ten assists in a clinching playoff loss to the Boston Celtics, his last game as a Cavalier for four seasons.

July 8, 2010: Announces on live TV that he is "taking his talents to South Beach" to play for the Miami Heat.

June 12, 2011: Heat loses to the Dallas Mavericks in the NBA Finals.

June 21, 2012: Wins his first NBA championship, versus the Oklahoma City Thunder.

June 20, 2013: Wins second NBA title, versus the San Antonio Spurs, with the Miami Heat.

September 14, 2013: Marries Savannah Brinson.

June 15, 2014: Heat lose to the Spurs in the NBA Finals.

July 11, 2014: Announces he is "coming home" to the Cavaliers.

June 16, 2015: Cavaliers lose to the Golden State Warriors in the NBA Finals.

June 19, 2016: Wins third NBA championship, versus the Warriors with the Cavaliers.

Glossary

Black Lives Matter Created after the murder of seventeen-year-old Trayvon Martin, the movement is a call to action and a response to the anti-black racism that is felt throughout society, working to affirm the contributions and the difference black people make every day.

derided To talk or write about someone or something in a very critical or insulting way; to laugh at or mock.

derogatorily Expressing a low opinion of or a lack of respect for someone or something.

emboldened Give someone the courage or confidence to do something or to behave in a certain way.

enigmatic Full of mystery and difficult to understand, puzzling.

entrepreneur One who organizes and manages any enterprise, especially a business, usually with considerable initiative and risk.

firestorm A large amount of anger and criticism.

hastening To cause something to happen more quickly.

icon A person who is very successful and admired or is considered representative of something.

idiom An expression whose meaning has come to mean something that is not predictable based on the words individually; the words as a group have come to have special meaning.

indict To formally decide that someone should be put on trial for a crime.

in effigy In public, a crude image or representation of a hated person.

logo A symbol or design that organizations adopt to identify their products. The NBA uses the recognizable silhouette basketball pose of Hall of Famer Jerry West of the Lakers as its logo.

obliterating To remove utterly from recognition or memory; to do away with or destroy completely.

parquet A surface (such as a floor) made of small pieces of wood that fit together to form a pattern.

perks Something extra that someone receives, because of your unique situation, in addition to regular pay for doing a job.

rancor Bitter, long-lasting resentment; deep-seated ill will.

regimen A plan or set of rules about food, exercise, etc., to make someone become or stay healthy.

reminiscent Reminding you of someone or something else; awakening memories of something similar.

resonates To have particular meaning or importance for someone; to affect or appeal to someone in a personal or emotional way.

rife Of common or frequent occurrence, often of something bad or unpleasant.

shill To talk about or describe someone or something in a favorable way because you are being paid to do it.

staple Used, needed, or enjoyed constantly by many people.

stick-to-itiveness The quality that allows someone to continue trying to do something even though it is difficult to accomplish.

transcendent Going beyond the limits of ordinary experience.

uncensored A publication, film, letter, etc., that has not been banned or edited.

Versaclimber A piece of equipment that combines both lower- and upper-body exercise into one vertical climbing motion machine.

vitriol Harsh and angry words, as in criticism.

Bibliography

Online Articles

Amato, Laura. "LeBron James' Kids: 5 Fast Facts You Need to Know." Heavy.com. June 9, 2015. http://heavy.com/sports/2015/06/lebron-james-kids-children-family-sons-daughter-savannah-brinson

Beaven, Michael. "LeBron James Family Foundation donates uniforms to Firestone athletes." *Akron Beacon Journal*. September 16, 2016. http://www.ohio.com/sports/high-school/city-series/lebron-james-family-foundation-donates-uniforms-to-firestone-athletes-1.712167

(Cleveland) *Plain Dealer* staff. "In everywhere but Miami, reaction to LeBron James' decision overwhelmingly negative: National media links." Cleveland.com. July 8, 2010. http://www.cleveland.com/cavs/index.ssf/2010/07/as_lebron_james_leaves_clevela.html

David, Mark. "LeBron James Snags Brentwood Mansion for $21 Million (EXCLUSIVE)." *Variety*. November 10, 2015. http://variety.com/2015/dirt/real-estalker/lebron-james-buys-brentwood-manse-1201635639/

DuPree, David. "NBA finally calls LeBron's number – No. 1," USATODAY.com, June 26, 2003. http://usatoday30.usatoday.com/sports/basketball/draft/2003-06-26-draft_x.htm

ESPN staff. "Is LeBron James the best athlete in the world?" ESPN.com. June 15, 2015. http://www.espn.com/nba/playoffs/2015/story/_/id/13037507/lebron-james-world-best-athlete

Hampton, Rickey L. Sr. "LeBron Building A Championship Legacy On And Off The Court." SportsBlog.com. Aug. 21, 2016. http://theafricanamericanathlete.sportsblog.com/posts/24058971/lebron-building-a-championship-legacy-on-and-off-the-court.html

Knowlton, Emmett. "LeBron James' business partner confirms lifetime deal with Nike is worth over $1 billion," *Business Insider*, May 17, 2016. http://www.businessinsider.com/lebron-james-nike-deal-exceeds-1-billion-maverick-carter-says-2016-5

"Life is all business for prep star LeBron James," *Charlotte Observer*, July 13, 2002. http://billingsgazette.com/sports/life-is-all-business-for-prep-star-lebron-james/article_c71e0be2-ec91-5dda-84c5-e4ba5f374b9c.html

McMillen, Matt. "LeBron James Pays Homage to the Mothers in His life." WebMD. April 22, 2010. http://www.webmd.com/parenting/features/lebron-james-pays-homage-to-the-mothers-in-his-life?page=4#1

Robson, Dan. "I Promise To Never Forget Where I Came From," Sportsnet.ca, 2014. http://www.sportsnet.ca/basketball/lebron-james-akron-ohio

Shontell, Alyson. "The Lebron James Interview: The world's best athlete reveals how his team pulled off the greatest comeback in NBA history." *Business Insider*, August 19, 2016. http://www.businessinsider.com/lebron-james-interview-space-jam-2-cavs-beating-the-warriors-and-philanthropy-2016-8

Slane, Kevin. "Mark Wahlberg and LeBron James are talking about making a movie together," Boston.com. September 21, 2016. http://www.boston.com/culture/entertainment/2016/09/21/mark-wahlberg-and-lebron-james-are-talking-about-making-a-movie-together

"Timeline of significant events in LeBron James' life," Ohio.com, July 11, 2014. http://www.ohio.com/news/local/timeline-of-significant-events-in-lebron-james-life-1.503649

Tobias, Scott. "LeBron James and Coach Dru Joyce." avclub.com. September 30, 2009. http://www.avclub.com/article/lebron-james-and-coach-dru-joyce-33524

Vardon, Joe. "LeBron James's Uninterrupted gets $15.8M investment from Warner Bros., Turner Sports," Cleveland.com, December 2, 2015. http://www.cleveland.com/cavs/index.ssf/2015/12/lebron_james_uninterrupted_get.html

———— "LeBron on Tamir Rice: 'This issue is bigger than me,' " Cleveland.com, December 30, 2015. http://www.cleveland.com/cavs/index.ssf/2015/12/lebron_on_tamir_rice_this_issu.html

Yuscavage, Chris. "LeBron James Talks Owning NBA Team and Michael Jordan's Legacy on New Podcast." Complex.com, August 17, 2016. http://www.complex.com/sports/2016/08/lebron-james-dream-own-nba-team

Further Information

Books

James, LeBron, Buzz Bissinger. *Shooting Stars*. New York: Penguin Press, 2009.

Joyce, Dru II. *Beyond Championships: A Playbook for Winning at Life*. Grand Rapids, Mich.: Zondervan, 2014.

McKee, Vince. *All In: The Story of LeBron James and the 2016 NBA Champion Cleveland Cavaliers*. New York: Sports Publishing, 2016.

Meale, Tony. *The Chosen Ones; The Team That Beat LeBron*. Cincinnati: Press Box Publishing, 2012.

Morgan, David Lee Jr. *LeBron James: The Rise of a Star*. Cleveland: Gray & Company, 2003.

Organizations

The LeBron James Family Foundation

http://lebronjamesfamilyfoundation.org
The official site of the foundation started by LeBron James provides updates on its many charitable ventures as well as messages from its founder.

NBA

http://www.nba.com
The National Basketball Association's official website provides links to all things basketball.

Sportrac

http://www.spotrac.com/nba/rankings/earnings/
This site is the largest online sports team and player contract resource available.

St. Vincent-St. Mary basketball arena website

http://www.stvm.com/athletics/lebron_james_arena.php
This site run by St. Vincent-St. Mary High School provides background information on its famous alumni as well as photos and items on its current players.

Video

Championship Parade and Rally: LeBron James — June 22, 2016

http://www.nba.com/cavaliers/video/teams/caval
iers/2016/06/23/1466706317717-160622-lebron-
championshiprally.mp4-611613
LeBron James praising his teammates at the parade in downtown Cleveland to celebrate the Cavaliers' 2016 NBA championship.

July 8, 2010 — ESPN — LeBron James "The Decision" Full Interview

https://www.youtube.com/watch?v=bHSLw8DLm20
LeBron James announcing his "decision" to join Dwyane Wade and Chris Bosh with the Miami Heat, in a live interview on ESPN in July 2010.

LeBron James' Historic Block on Andre Iguodala From All Angles

http://www.nba.com/video/channels/playoffs/
finals/2016/06/22/lebron-james-big-block-on-iggy-game7.nba
LeBron James comes from nowhere to block Andre Iguodala at a crucial point in Game Seven of the 2016 NBA Finals won by his Cleveland Cavaliers.

Miami Heat Welcome Party

https://www.youtube.com/watch?v=e9BqUBYaHlM
LeBron James saying the Miami Heat will win "not one, not two, not three, not four, not five, not six, not seven …" NBA championships with his teammates Dwyane Wade and Chris Bosh.

NBA Stars Call for an End to Violence

http://espn.go.com/video/clip?id=17061524
LeBron James, Dwyane Wade, Chris Paul, and Carmelo Anthony at the 2016 ESPYS talking about stopping the violence against black men and law enforcement.

Index

Page numbers in **boldface** are illustrations. Entries in **boldface** are glossary terms.

acting career, 92–94
Akron I Promise, 7, 85
Akron, 6–7, **8**, 10, 12, 14–15, 24, 40, 44, 54, 61, 65–68, 83–85, 90, 95–96
Anthony, Carmelo, 31, **33**, 46, 72, 89
autobiography (*Shooting Stars*), 10–11, 17, 84

Black Lives Matter, 89
Bosh, Chris, 31, 43, 47, 51–54, **52**, 57, 61, 63, 65, 72
Boston Celtics, 37, 46, 70
Brown, Mike, 35

Cleveland, 5–6, **8**, 18, 23, 28, 31, 37–38, 41, 44, 46, 50–51, 54, 65–66, 68–69, 77–79, 87, 91–92, 94
Cleveland Cavaliers (Cavs), 5, 24, 27–28, 31–32, 34–39, 41, 43–46, 49–50, 54, **55**, 59, 66–70, 72, 74–75, 78–79, 81, 86, 90–91, 95, 97
Cotton, Sian, 12, 24

Curry, Stephen, 77

derided, 68
derogatorily, 44

emboldened, 89
enigmatic, 5
entrepreneur, 7

"Fab Four," 12, 14, 18
firestorm, 54

Gilbert, Dan, 49, 67–68

hastening, 66

icon, 65, 83
idiom, 53
in effigy, 5
indict, 87
Irving, Kyrie, 69, 72, 74–75, 77–79, 87
Iverson, Allen, 11, 29

James, Savannah Brinson, 15, 49, 61
Johnson, Magic, 20, 32, 35, 90
Jordan, Michael, 5–6, 11, 29, 43–44, 51, 83, 90, 92

Joyce, "Coach Dru," 11–12, 15, 17, 23–24, 40
Joyce, "Little Dru," 11–12, 14, 24, 40

LeBron James Family Foundation, 83–84
logo, 29
Love, Kevin, 69, 72, 74
Lucas, John, 27

McGee, Willie, 12, 24
Miami Heat, 31, 43, 45, 54, 74, 87
Miami, 44, 51, 57–58, 62, 65–68, 79
More Than a Game, 40
Most Valuable Player (MVP), 14, 35, 39, 41, 54, 56, 58–59, 61, 77–78, 95
mother/mom, 6, 9–10, 21, 23, 28, 31, 39, 45, 66, 84, 86

NBA, 5–7, 11, 21, 25, 27, 29–31, 34–36, 38–40, 43, 47, 49, 51, 54, 56–59, 61–63, 65, 69–70, 74–75, 78–79, 83, 86, 89–92, 95, 97
NBA finals, 6, 36, 47, 54, 58–59, 61–63, 65, 70, 74–75, 77–78, 92, 95
Northeast Ohio Shooting Stars, 12

Obliterating, 38
Ohio High School Athletic Association (OHSAA), 21, 23
Olympic basketball team, 34, 37
O'Neal, Shaquille, 41

parquet, 41
Paxson, Jim, **26**, 27–28, 32
perks, 96
Popovich, Gregg, 36, 59, 63

rancor, 45
Reed, John, 11
regimen, 91
reminiscent, 20
resonates, 85
rife, 70
Riley, Pat, 44, 52, 67
Rookie of the Year, 5, 34, 95

shill, 20
Silas, Paul, 35
social activism, 86–90, **88**
South Beach, 5, 43, 45, 51, 65
Spoelstra, Erik, 52–53, 56, 62
Sports Illustrated, 6, 17, 34, 51, 66, 83, 95
staple, 86
Stern, David, **30**, 31, 49
stick-to-itiveness, 36

St. Vincent-St. Mary High
    School (SVSM), 7, **13**,
    14–15, 17, **19**, 20–21, 24–25,
    28, 39

transcendent, 67
Travis, Romeo, 14, 24

uncensored, 93
Uninterrupted (website), 91,
    93–94

VersaClimber, 91
vitriol, 50

Wade, Dwyane, 31, 43, 46–47,
    51, **52**, 53–54, 56, 58, 63, 65,
    72, 89
Walker, Frankie, 10–11, 24

About the Author

Rachel Shuster is the editor at the Washington, DC-based Tax Foundation following a lengthy career as a sportswriter, columnist, and sports editor. She was the NBA editor at *USA Today* when LeBron James made his move from Cleveland to Miami. Shuster was a founding employee at *USA Today* and has covered the Super Bowl, World Series, Olympics, Stanley Cup Finals, the Masters, Wimbledon, and even the National Rodeo Finals. She was the first woman to be a national sports columnist.